CH00661878

Get Your Crochet On!
FLY TOPS & FUNKY FLAVAS

Afya Ibomu

Photography by Shannon McCollum
and Charles Beard

The Taunton Press

To all crochet designers who want
to write their own books. You can do it!

© 2007 by Afya Ibomu
All rights reserved.

The Taunton Press, Inc., 63 South Main Street, PO Box 5506, Newtown, CT 06470-5506
e-mail: tp@taunton.com

Editor: Pam Hoenig
Layout: Cathy Cassidy
Illustrators: Christine Erikson; Marcus Williams (pp. 4–41)
Photographers: Shannon McCollum and Charles Beard

Library of Congress Cataloging-in-Publication Data
Ibomu, Afya.
  Get your crochet on! fly tops & funky flavas / author, Afya Ibomu ; photographer, Shannon McCollum and Charles Beard.
     p. cm. -- (Get your crochet on!)
  Includes index.
  ISBN 978-1-56158-941-8
  1. Crocheting--Patterns. 2. Dress accessories. I. Title.

TT825.I22 2007
746.43'4041--dc22

                    2007010140

Printed in Singapore
10 9 8 7 6 5 4 3 2 1

The following manufacturers/names appearing in *Get Your Crochet On!* are trademarks: Bernat®,
Hobby Lobby℠, Lion Brand Yarns®, Michaels℠, Patons®, Red Heart®, Reynolds®, Wal-Mart℠

Shout Outs!

I want to give thanks to my family for their love and support!

To my husband, Khnum, you have a brilliant mind! Thanks for your patience, help, support and understanding. I love you!

To Itwela, my little man, you are so strong, creative, and beautiful! Thank you for your design and color inspirations. I love you!

Thanks to the two women who helped decode and check my patterns: Beverly Thompson and my mom, Carolyn Sanders (I love you). I could not have done it without you!

To Regina, my literary agent from Serendipity Literary Agency, we did it again. You are the greatest!

Shannon McCollum, my road dog and photographer extraordinaire. Thanks for your eye and helping to bring my vision to life.

I also want to thank everyone else who helped this book happen:

Instructional Photographer: Charles Beard (www.visionsbycharles.com)
Illustrator: Marcus Williams (www.staybattlin.com)
Fashion Stylist: Kasema Kalifah (www.kasemakalifah.com)
Stylist Assistant: Jamila Palmer
Second Assistant: Lola
Makeup Artist: Jamika Crowner, Fantasy Faces Makeup Artistry
(www.myspace.com/fantasy_faces)

Models:

Zayd Akinyela

Z. Jaha Asante (earthmotherpress.com; myspace.com/realblakgirlsruletheworld)

Erykah Badu

Mike Flo
(mikeflo.com, myspace.com/404mikeflo)

Quinton Garrin

Jada Mister

Jamila Messiah

Damineke Ramsey

Sabrina Rose (Slick & Rose;
www.myspace.com/slickandrose)

Kat Slatery (breakdancer)

Sticman
(Dead Prez; www.bossupbu.com)

Adria Wiley

Celia Faussart

Photographer: A. Louis

Stylist: Shana Jackson

Contents

Introduction

. . . .

Get Your Crochet On! Fly Tops & Funky Flavas features tank tops, tunics, jewelry, belts, and more. The second installment of the *Get Your Crochet On!* series continues with vibrant colors; simple stitches; and easy-to-follow patterns, illustrations, and instructional photos. These patterns offer something for every skill level. Men, women, and teens will enjoy stylin' in these 30 original designs!

My goal for this book is to bring crochet *Back to the Future.* I grabbed inspiration from rock music, '80s hip hop, and Native and African crafts, then blended those with classic styles and futuristic funk!

There are also a few instructional sections that are new to this book, which will help guide you through reading patterns, organizing your yarn, and build your crochet skills.

So step in to the future and *Get Your Crochet On!*

Getting Started!

What You Need

The tools needed to crochet are few and basic—really, just a hook and some yarn. A couple of other items will allow you to give your projects a finished look.

Yarn

At some point in my crocheting life, I became a yarn fiend. I shop for yarn all over the country—at flea markets and in craft and yarn stores—but my favorite place to find yarn is thrift stores. Thrift stores have very inexpensive yarn. You can find unique, old-school yarn with distinctive colors that are no longer made. Color is such an important part of the art of crochet. The use of one subtle hue can transform an item and make it unique. It's fun to be creative with your color choices and to use your environment for inspiration.

My patterns can be made using many different types of yarn, **sport-weight** or **worsted-weight cotton** or **acrylic yarns. Worsted** yarns are medium-weight yarns and the most common kind. **Sport-weight** yarns are a little thinner, or lighter, than worsted-weight yarns. **Acrylic** yarns are synthetic but have a bulky feel similar to wool. They come in a very large selection of colors and are generally quite affordable. Acrylic and wool yarns are good to use in the fall and winter for warmth. Cotton yarn is softer than acrylic and comes in sport and worsted weights as well. Cotton can be used all year round. It will keep you cool in the summer, and you can layer with it in the winter.

While I was working on this book, I went on tour for my first book, *Hip Hats & Cool Caps*, and I found that many crocheters frown on the use of acrylic yarns. Personally, I like to use a mix of all types of yarns. I really like acrylic yarn because it is inexpensive and easy to use and most brands can be machine washed and thrown in the drier with minimal change in their size.

The great thing about the patterns in this book is that they allow you to choose the yarn you want, personalizing your piece.

I use **nylon yarn** to make shoestrings, belts, and earrings. It has a glossy sheen that is similar to some types of cotton yarn. Nylon gives your work a fancier look than acrylic yarn does, and it's as sturdy as acrylic without being as bulky. Nylon comes in two different thicknesses, which are comparable to sport- and worsted-weight acrylic.

Textured novelty yarns—which are made from a wide variety of synthetic and natural fibers—are great for adding flair to any item and come in many different weights and textures. Unfortunately, they are usually expensive and come in small skeins, and you have to buy a lot to make a basic-size top.

Crafter's rope (trim) has become my new favorite type of string to work with! I use it for belts and jewelry. It is very sturdy and comes in great metallic colors. You can usually find it in craft stores near the plastic canvas area. Unfortunately, the cord usually comes in only 10- or 20-yard skeins, which means you will have to buy at least 10 skeins to complete a project. That can end up being a little pricey, but the funkiness it adds to a project is really worth it.

Cross-stitch yarns and crochet thread are great for shoestrings and earrings. Crochet thread is easy to find and inexpensive. Cross-stitch yarn comes in small skeins but it comes in great colors and is reasonably priced.

Organizing your yarn

Organizing your yarn can help you come up with great color combinations, save you money (you won't go buying four skeins of yellow cotton yarn when you already have eight skeins packed away somewhere in the back of the closet), and can ease your mind from some of the overwhelming clutter that we yarn lovers sometimes face.

Because I am a Virgo, I have a natural tendency to be obsessively organized. I have my yarn organized by color and fiber. All of my acrylic and wool yarns are together and as are my cotton yarns. I have also added a small space for textured or novelty yarns because they can sometimes get lost among the larger skeins. I keep my leftover yarn and nylon yarn in a clear stackable bin with a lid.

Find a place and a method of storage that makes sense for your available space and usage. A closet, stackable crates, shelves, or clear bins can all work. See-through bins with lids are good for small skeins and leftover yarn. Make sure you can see the yarn clearly and that it's easily accessible.

Crocheting with double strands

In some of my patterns, I'll instruct you to crochet with two strands of yarn at once (the same yarn or two different yarns) for one of several reasons. First, the finished crocheted fabric is stiffer than it would be if you had used just one strand; this gives extra body to certain features, such as the chain in a piece of jewelry. Second, crocheting with two strands of yarn in different weights or colors will give you a unique color or texture effect. For example, if the top you're making is predominantly crocheted in worsted-weight yarn,

Worsted-weight yarn

Sport-weight yarn

Nylon yarn

Textured yarn

Metallic yarn

Crochet thread

Cross-stitch yarn

To crochet with double strands, either you can work from the skein and a separate small ball or you can crochet with both ends of the same skein.

but you want to use a particular sport-weight yarn for a section of it, crochet that portion with a double strand of the thinner yarn to get the same approximate weight as the worsted. Do the same thing if you are crocheting with a chunky yarn but want to use a favorite worsted yarn for part of it. Or, you can use a double strand for a whole project if the pattern asks for a heavy weight yarn but your yarn of choice is lighter in weight.

Each skein of yarn has two ends. One is on the outside of the skein; the other is located in the middle of the skein. It's preferable to use the end in the center, but you may have to dig into the middle through both ends of the skein to find it. To crochet with double strands, grab both the outside and the center ends, hold them together as one strand, and start crocheting. Or, you can roll a ball of yarn and use the ball and skein.

Hooks

The hook has a few distinct parts on it. The *tip* is inserted into the stitches. The *throat* hooks the yarn and pulls it through the stitch. The *shaft* holds the loops you're working with, and its thickness determines the size of your stitch. The *thumb res* allows you to rotate the hook easily as you make each stitch. The *handle* is used for balance and leverage to help keep the hook steady and for maneuvering it properly.

Everyone has a favorite type of hook to use, and if you're a beginner, it won't be long until you do, too. Each kind of hook has a different weight and feel in your hand, and some work better than others with particular kinds of yarn. The right hook is the one that feels best in your hand and works most effectively with the yarn you're using.

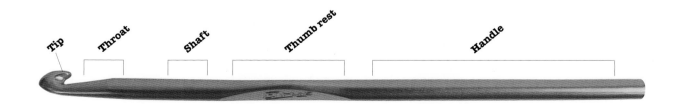

Tip   Throat   Shaft   Thumb rest   Handle

Plastic hooks are usually recommended for beginning crocheters. Lightweight and inexpensive, they work well with lighter yarns, like sport weight. Personally, they feel a little flimsy to me, and I've even broken a few when crocheting with double strands.

Aluminum hooks are very sturdy, reasonably priced, and one of the best types of hook to use when crocheting with double strands or chunky yarns. They also seem to make your stitch a slight bit tighter.

Wood and bamboo hooks are my personal favorites because of the way they feel in my hand. They're wonderful for working with sport- and worsted-weight yarns, but sometimes are not sturdy enough and the tips can be too narrow for crocheting with two strands.

Bone hooks feel great, but sometimes the tips are not very smooth, can catch on the yarn, and can cause fraying. They work better with lighter-weight yarns, like sport-weight cotton or crochet thread.

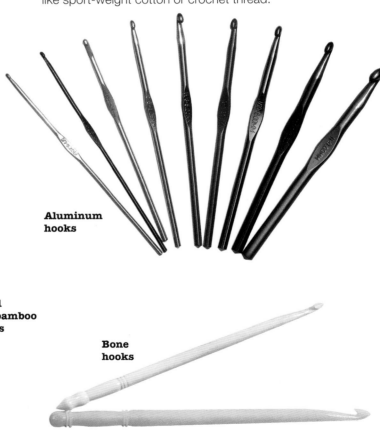

Plastic hooks

Aluminum hooks

Wood and bamboo hooks

Bone hooks

Hook sizes

The size of a crochet hook is based on its thickness, and it also corresponds to the weight of the yarn you're using. Lighter-weight yarns, like sport weight, require smaller-size hooks; thicker yarns, like chunky or doubled yarns, require larger hooks.

Hooks are measured by two different sizing systems. The American system is based on letters and numbers. The higher the number or the farther along the letter of the alphabet, the larger the hook. In the second system—based on the metric system and used in Europe and Canada—the hook width is measured in millimeters. The bigger the number, the thicker the hook. All the patterns in this book were crocheted with American hooks; but in the instructions, I will give the suggested hook sizes in both American and metric figures, so you're covered no matter what's available in your area. And even if you're using the recommended size hook for a given project, always remember to check your gauge before starting and to adjust your hook size if necessary (see page 34 for more on this).

Crochet Hook Size Equivalents

American	Metric (mm)
B/1	2.25 mm
C/2	2.75 mm
D/3	3.25 mm
E/4	3.5 mm
F/5	3.75 mm
G/6	4.0 mm
H/8	5.0 mm
I/9	5.5 mm
J/10	6.0 mm
K/10	6.5 mm
N	9.0 mm
P	10.0 mm
Q	15.0 mm

Additional Tools

Some basic sewing and craft tools are needed to finish your projects. Most of these items can be found in craft stores or the notions section of a fabric store.

Foil tape
Foil tape secures shoestring ends. It can be found at most hardware stores.

Embroidery needles

Weaving needles

A selection of embroidery and weaving needles comes in handy for weaving in yarn ends and adding elastic for a snug fit.

Cabone rings

Cabone rings are used for earring hoops. They can be found in the notions section of craft or fabric stores.

Thread

Swivel hooks/cobra key chains
Swivel hooks and cobra key chains are used as jewelry clasps.

Sewing needles and thread will help secure snaps.

Fabric glue
Fabric glue can be used to secure yarn ends firmly and prevent unraveling.

Beads

Beads can be decorative accents to jewelry, tops, and accessories.

Tape measure
A tape measure is necessary for checking your gauge and measuring your work as you crochet.

Aleene's **STOP FRAYING** PREVENTS FABRICS & TRIMS

Plastic bangles

Steel bangles

Bangles, both steel and plastic, can be used as the foundation for bracelets and earring hoops.

Belt buckles
Belt buckles are best found in thrift stores, where you can buy them from 50 cents on up. To remove one from a belt, just use scissors to cut the buckle off. For the Steppin Out belt on page 82, you will need a large buckle with a bar across. Use pliers to remove the pin. For the Stay Up belt on page 66, a standard belt buckle will work; do not remove the pin.

Stitch markers

Stitch markers can help you keep count of your rows and stitches as you are working.

Round elastic
Round cord elastic (beading elastic) is used to enhance the fit of a top. It can be used round waists, necks, and sleeves to add shaping. It is found in the notions or beading section of fabric and craft stores.

Scissors
Scissors cut loose threads and tape.

Fishhook wires
Fishhook wires are used as earring hooks. They can be found in the jewelry section of craft stores.

Snaps
Snaps are needed for several projects. I like to use the larger sizes, between #4 and #10. They can be found in the notions section of fabric and craft stores.

Pliers
Pliers can take off the pins from recycled belts.

Color Inspirations

For this book I was inspired by native, cultural, and modern styles.

Choosing Colors

When thinking about the new projects for this book, I saw beautiful color combinations on album covers, the sides of buildings, and in the pages of home decor catalogs. I made color swatches whenever I saw a color combination that I liked. I would grab yarns that had the closest colors to what I saw, snip pieces off with scissors, tie them in a loose knot, and save them. Then when I wanted to make something, I would have that swatch to refer to.

But choosing colors can also be as simple as picking your favorite color or trying to match an outfit. I have always been inspired by nature and the world around me. Each season has its own color scheme with its own energy. Here are a few colors that correspond to each season.

- **Spring:** Pastels, such as pink and light green, baby blue and yellow
- **Summer:** Red, orange, yellow, turquoise, blue, bright green and sand
- **Autumn:** Amber, orange, brown, and green
- **Winter:** Gray, winter white, black, and blue

From Inspiration to Crochet

Spring

Spring colors

Summer

Summer colors

Autumn

Autumn colors

Winter

Winter colors

The Color Wheel and Basic Color Theory

Using a color wheel will help you choose a pleasing mix of colors as well as open your mind to color combinations that you may not have thought of using. Please refer to and use the color wheel at *direction* to help you with your selections.

The primary colors are yellow, red, and blue. These are the colors that cannot be made by mixing other colors.

The secondary colors are those made by combining primary colors. They are:

- Red + blue = violet (purple)
- Blue + yellow = green
- Yellow + red = orange

The tertiary colors are a mix of one primary color and one of the secondary colors next to it on the color wheel. The six tertiary colors are:

- Blue + green = turquoise
- Green + yellow = lime green
- Violet + red = crimson
- Red + orange = red-orange
- Yellow + orange = yellow-orange
- Blue + violet = blue-violet

Color Wheel Crochet

Primary Colors

Secondary Colors

Tertiary Colors

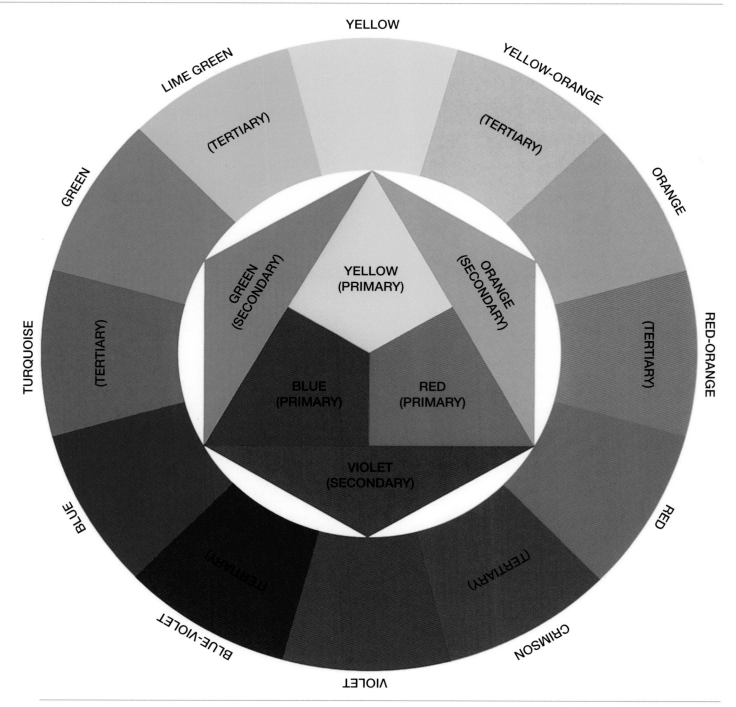

YELLOW

YELLOW-ORANGE

(TERTIARY)

LIME GREEN

(TERTIARY)

ORANGE

GREEN

YELLOW
(PRIMARY)

GREEN
(SECONDARY)

ORANGE
(SECONDARY)

RED-ORANGE

TURQUOISE

(TERTIARY)

BLUE
(PRIMARY)

RED
(PRIMARY)

(TERTIARY)

VIOLET
(SECONDARY)

RED

BLUE

(TERTIARY)

(TERTIARY)

BLUE-VIOLET

CRIMSON

VIOLET

How to Read a Crochet Pattern

This section is for the many people who have said that they love my designs but don't know how to read a pattern. Being able to read a pattern allows you to improve your crocheting skills and techniques, learn how to make new things, and design your own patterns that you can make over and over again.

The Parts of a Pattern

Reading and understanding a pattern can be a little intimidating, but you don't have to be a math whiz to figure it out. Once you familiarize yourself with the abbreviations, reading a pattern can become as simple as reading a recipe.

Supplies and materials

Each pattern has a section that tells you what you'll need to make the project: the type and amount of yarn; the hook size; and any other supplies, such as elastic, weaving needles, and stitch markers.

Gauge

Gauge is important because it allows you to make the correct-size item. The gauge is the number of stitches you should have per inch when crocheting a pattern with the particular yarn and hook specified.

It usually looks like this: 16 dc = 4"

This specific example means this: if you crochet 16 double crochet stitches in a row, the row should measure 4 inches. If you work 16 double crochet stitches and your piece measures more than 4 inches, then you crochet looser than the person who made the pattern. To obtain the gauge listed, use a series of hooks in smaller sizes until you find one that gives you the same gauge called for in the pattern. On the other hand, if you work 16 double crochet stitches and your

piece measures less than 4 inches, then you crochet tighter than the person who made the pattern. To correct for this, you should try crocheting with a series of hooks in larger sizes until you achieve gauge. For more on the importance of gauge, see page 34.

Sizes

The measurements tell you what your size options are for the pattern. But just as a size small top in one name brand may fit you differently from the same size top in another brand, so it is with crochet patterns. To be safe, measure yourself; then look at the measurements on the project's schematic to find the size you'd like to make. Personally, I like to wear my clothes a little tight, so I start with a smaller size. Whichever way you like to wear your clothes is the way you should choose your size, bigger or smaller.

Schematic

The schematic is a drawing that shows the finished measurements in inches of the different sizes of the pattern.

Special stitches

Special stitches are either different from the basic stitches (sc, hdc, dc, tr) or are a group of stitches to be worked together (for example, [2 dc, ch1, 2 dc] in the next stitch).

Crochet Abbreviations

All crochet patterns use abbreviations in their directions.
Here are the ones you'll come across in this book.

ch(s)	chain(s)	sl	slip
ch sp	chain space	sl st	slip stitch
cl	cluster	sp(s)	space(s)
dc	double crochet	st(s)	stitch(es)
dec	decrease	tr	triple or treble crochet
ea	each	yd	yard(s)
g	gram(s)	yo	yarn over
hdc	half double crochet	WS(s)	wrong side(s)
oz	ounce(s)	*	asterisk is used to mark the beginning of a part of the instructions that will be worked more than once
rep	repeat		
rnd(s)	round(s)		
RS(s)	right side(s)	( )	parentheses
sc	single crochet	[ ]	brackets
sk	skip		

The directions

The directions are written in a sort of shorthand code of abbreviations and are usually organized in rows or rounds (rnds).

Abbreviations

Crochet patterns are abbreviated to keep the patterns short and simple. For example, "2 dc in next 2 sts, 3 sc in next st" means make "two double crochets in the next two stitches, three single crochets in next stitch." Once you learn what the abbreviations mean, it just takes a little patience and you will be crocheting in no time!

Parentheses

Parentheses can mean many things. They are used for separating the instructions or measurements for the different sizes, for example:

small(medium,large): sc in next 8(10,12) sts

In this case, the parentheses help to set apart the different sizes you can make with the pattern. If you are making a medium, you would follow the numbers corresponding to the placement of the word *medium*, which is 10 stitches.

At the end of a row or round, you may see a number of stitches set in parentheses or brackets, for example:

(30 sts)

In this case, the parentheses are setting off the number of stitches you should have at the end of that row or round. If there are several numbers, they are the stitch counts for the different sizes given in the pattern.

Last, you will sometimes see stitch combinations set in parentheses; these are stitches that are meant to be worked as a group into one stitch or worked as in combination and then repeated, for example:

(1 dc in next 5 sts, 2 dc in next st) 3 times

This means that you crochet the combination of stitches within the parentheses for a total of three times within your row or round.

Brackets

Brackets can be used interchangeably with parentheses to separate or contain repeating stitches within a row or round, for example:

[1 dc, 2 dc in next st] 3 times

This means that you crochet the combination of stitches within the brackets for a total of three times. Brackets can also be located outside or inside parentheses when a smaller section is repeated within a larger section, for example:

(1 sc in next st, [2 sc in next st, ch 1] twice) 2 times

This means that you first make a single crochet in the next stitch and then you repeat the sequence within the brackets two times. Finally, you repeat the entire combination within the parentheses again.

U.S. or UK?

American and British patterns use two different crochet languages. All the patterns in this book were written in U.S. terms.

U.S. TERM	UK TERM
Slip stitch	Single crochet
Single crochet	Double crochet
Half double crochet	Half treble
Double crochet	Treble
Triple/triple	Double treble
Double treble crochet	Triple/treble treble

The Meaning of Right and Wrong

When a pattern refers to the right side (like in, "with right sides facing") it means the outside, or public side, of the item—the side that is meant to be seen. The wrong side, or the inside, is the side that is not meant to be seen and the side you'll want to weave your yarn ends into.

Asterisks

Asterisks indicate that you need to repeat a group of stitches. They come in pairs and may be located at the beginning or the end of a pattern repeat, such as:

*(1 sc in next 2 sts, 2 sc in next st, 1 sc in next 2 sts), rep from * 3 times

This means that you crochet the combination within the parentheses once and then repeat that sequence three more times.

Commas, semicolons and periods

A comma or semicolon usually indicates that something is changing in a section. A period lets you know that a section is finished.

The Sizing of the Patterns in this Book

I had two very wonderful, patient women help me check the patterns. Despite their patience, they both found they had difficulty following the stitch counts and measurements for their particular size. For this reason, I came up with the idea to color code the different sizes to allow you to easily recognize where you are in the pattern. The size colors are consistent throughout all of the patterns and are indicated here and at the beginning of each pattern.

X-small	Large
Small	X-large
Medium	XX-large

Throughout the pattern you will be able to follow along working with only the color for your size, for example:

Rnds 3–24(3–24,3–26,3–27,3–28,3–30):

Ch 4, turn, *(sk next ch sp, 1 dc in next dc, ch 2), rep from * 18(18,20,22,23,24) times. 20(20,23,24,25, 26) dc]

Having Problems with a Pattern?

All of these patterns have been checked and rechecked by me, two pattern checkers, an editor, and a copyeditor; but sometimes mistakes can happen. If a pattern is not working out, please check my website, www.getyourcrochet.com, for corrections. If you notice any mistake, please email me at info@nattral.com so that I can post it online.

Level of Difficulty

Each pattern is labeled by its level of dificulty:

1 Young buck (beginner): Great for those new to crocheting or reading pattern

11 Some skills (intermediate): You have followed and made some patterns successfully

111 Mad skills (advanced): You have been following patterns for years

The Basics

In this section, I'm going to cover what you need to know to make the patterns in this book. You'll learn how to hold a crochet hook, how make all the stitches called for in the patterns, and some other useful techniques.

Making a slip knot

Every crocheted project begins with a slip knot.
After you make it, slip it onto your hook.

1. Loop the yarn around your index finger and grab the yarn with your thumb and middle finger.

2. Bring the yarn behind and around the loop.

3. Pull the end of the yarn through the loop.

4. Pull the yarn gently.

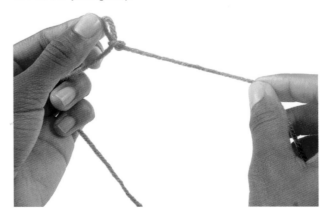

Holding Your Crochet Hook

There are two ways you can hold the hook, and which you choose is simply a matter of your own personal comfort.

You can hold the hook like a pencil • • •

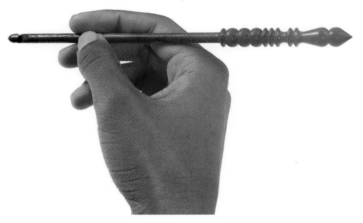

• • • **or** you can hold it like a knife.

Holding the Yarn

First, make a slip knot and place it on your hook. Hold the hook in your dominant hand.

1. With your fingers spread, drape the yarn over the last three fingers and behind the index finger of your other hand.

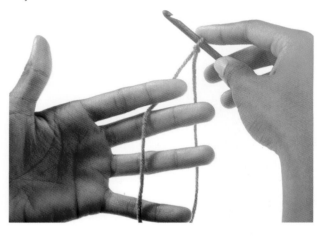

2. Bring the yarn over your index finger and hold it between your thumb and middle finger.

As you crochet, you need to secure the yarn in your hand to add some tension or you'll be crocheting very loosely. You can either:

Hold the yarn loosely with your pinky and ring finger • • •

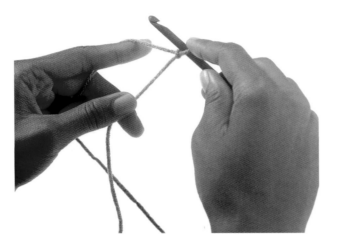

• • • **or** wrap the yarn around your pinkie (do whichever feels best).

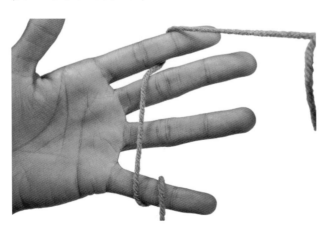

Yarn Over (yo)

The yarn over is one of the most basic techniques in crocheting. It is a component of every crochet stitch.

To yarn over, wrap the yarn over your hook from back to front (clockwise), then proceed as directed by the pattern.

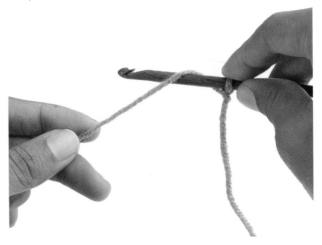

Chain Stitch (ch)

Make a slip knot and place it on your hook.

Grab the yarn with the hook (moving the hook around the yarn clockwise) and pull it through the slip knot.

For a chain stitch, grab the yarn and pull it through.

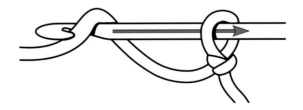

Working into the Front or Back of a Stitch

Working into the front or the back loop of a stitch instead of picking up both threads creates a raised, textured look.

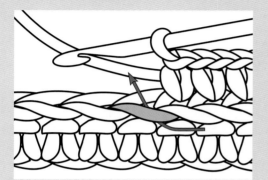

Crocheting into the front loop of a stitch.

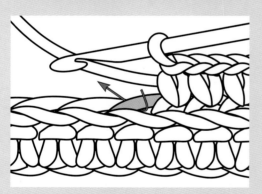

Crocheting into the back loop of a stitch.

Counting chain stitches:

Always start with the first chain away from the hook and count toward the start of the chain. Do not count the slip knot or the loop presently on the hook as part of the chain.

The sides of the chain

Just like the right or wrong side of a top, the chain stitch also has a right and wrong side. You will usually be crocheting into the right side.

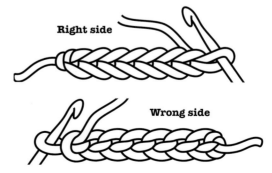

Right side

Wrong side

Slip Stitch (sl st)

Insert your hook into a stitch or space as directed, yarn over, and pull the yarn through the stitch and the loop on the hook.

Single Crochet (sc)

Insert your hook into a stitch or space as directed, yarn over (figure 1), and pull the yarn through the stitch; you now have two loops on the hook. Yarn over and pull yarn through both loops (figure 2).

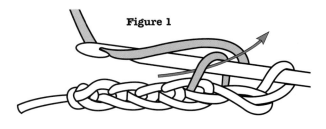

Figure 1

Figure 2

Half Double Crochet (hdc)

Yarn over, insert the hook into a stitch or space as directed, yarn over (figure 3), and pull yarn through the stitch; you now have three loops on the hook. Yarn over and pull yarn through all three loops on the hook (figure 4).

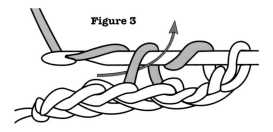

Figure 3

Figure 4

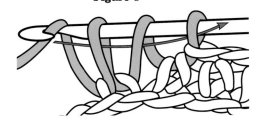

Double Crochet (dc)

Yarn over, insert the hook into a stitch or space as directed, yarn over, and pull yarn through the stitch; you now have three loops on the hook. Yarn over and pull yarn through the first two loops on the hook (figure 5); you now have two loops on the hook. Yarn over again and pull yarn through the last two loops on the hook (figure 6).

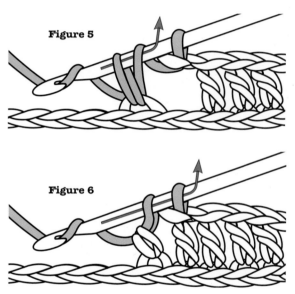

Figure 5

Figure 6

Triple (or Treble) Crochet (tr)

Yarn over two times, insert the hook into a stitch or space as directed, yarn over, and pull yarn through the stitch (figure 7); you now have four loops on the hook. Yarn over and pull yarn through the first two loops on the hook (figure 8); you now have three loops on the hook. Yarn over again and pull yarn through the next two loops on the hook; you now have two loops on the hook. Yarn over again and pull yarn through the last two loops on the hook (figure 9).

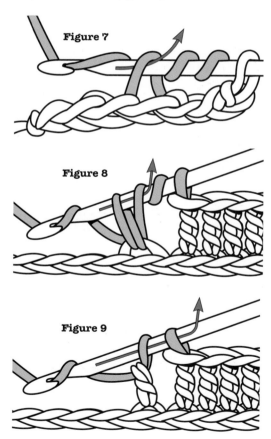

Figure 7

Figure 8

Figure 9

Working in Rows

All crochet projects start with a foundation chain. Once you've gotten the proper number of stitches in your chain (see Counting Chain Stitches on page 25), you will crochet back into each of the chain stitches using whatever stitch your pattern calls for.

Before beginning the next row, you'll make one or more chain stitches (your pattern will tell you how many; for example, ch 1 means to make 1 chain stitch), then flip the piece over, or turn, so that you can work back across the row. The chain stitch or stitches is called the *turning chain*.

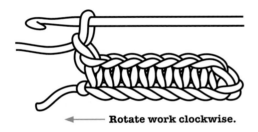

← Rotate work clockwise.

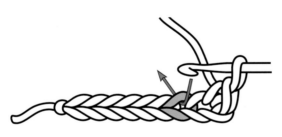

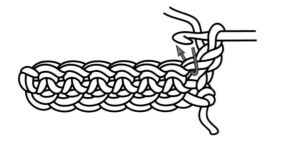

Which stitch to begin with in a row

Your pattern will tell you which stitch on a row to begin with. For example, it might say, "Sc into 1st st from hook," meaning you'll work a single crochet into the first stitch away from your hook. "Dc into 2nd st from hook," means you'll work a double crochet into the second stitch away from your hook.

Working in first stitch from hook.

Working in second stitch from hook.

Unless you're otherwise directed, to crochet into a stitch you'll insert your hook under the top two threads of the stitch (as shown below).

Follow the pattern directions to the end of the row, chain 1, and continue.

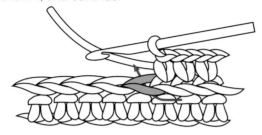

Working in Rounds

Begin a round like you begin a row: make a chain, but instead of crocheting back into the chain, you'll join one end of it to the other using a slip stitch to create a ring. Then, like working in rows, you work a chain for the first stitch, then crochet however many stitches are required into the center of the ring *not* into the chain stitches themselves.

When you get to the end of the round, join the front of the round with the end of it before going on to the next round. Do this by making a slip stitch into the top of the first stitch of the round. To work the next round, you'll be instructed to chain, then work into the individual stitches and/or spaces.

Now You See It, Now You Don't

When the wrong sides of the panels are facing each other, the seam will be on the right side (the public side) of the piece. When the right sides are facing each other, the seam will appear on the wrong side (the inside) of the piece.

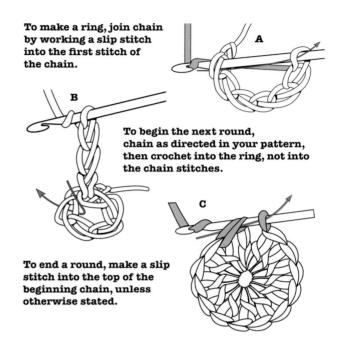

To make a ring, join chain by working a slip stitch into the first stitch of the chain.

A

B

To begin the next round, chain as directed in your pattern, then crochet into the ring, not into the chain stitches.

C

To end a round, make a slip stitch into the top of the beginning chain, unless otherwise stated.

For a cleaner join: Sometimes your joins can look a little sloppy and show a diagonal seam throughout the garment. Try this technique to correct it. Work a round and, before joining, take out your hook and insert it, left to right, into the stitch you want to join, then into the loop you just dropped. Pull the loop (instead of the working chain) through the stitch and continue.

Joining from back to front

Working in continuous rounds

Working in continuous rounds (also known as working in a spiral) allows for a cleaner, more finished look. Instead of joining your last stitch to your first stitch or chain, you will continue working into the next round. Use a stitch marker to keep track of the beginning of each round. Tip: When you get to the chain stitch, work a sc into it to reduce the hole that may appear, then continue working the stitch continued in the pattern.

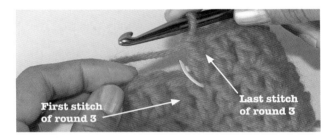

First stitch of round 3

Last stitch of round 3

Do not join.

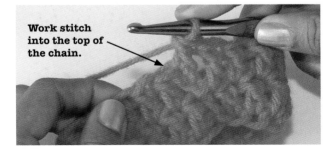

Work stitch into the top of the chain.

Which stitch to begin with in a round

As with working in rows, you may be instructed to start each round in a specific stitch (for example, the first or second stitch from the hook). If no stitch is specified, assume you'll begin in the first stitch.

Working into the first stitch from the hook.

Working in second stitch from hook.

Count your stitches

It's very important that you check your stitch count at the end of every row to make sure you haven't skipped or added any stitches. If you don't count for a couple of rows or rounds and find out you've got the wrong number of stitches, it's going to be difficult to figure out where you made the mistake. Using the stitch markers can help you keep track of your stitches and rows.

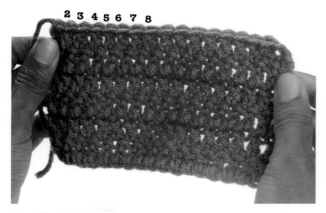

Counting stitches in a row.

Counting stitches in a round.

Increasing and Decreasing

Sometimes it may be necessary to increase or decrease within a row or round. Increasing and decreasing are used to change the shape of a garment and improve the fit. For instance, in the Sporties sock pattern on page 68, you will decrease so that the sock will fit snug around your calf and ankle.

Increasing within a round or row

Work two or more stitches into the same stitch in the beginning, middle, or end of a round or row.

Increasing in beginning of row

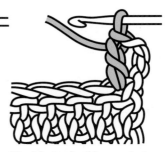

Working a double crochet increase at the beginning of a row.

Increasing in row

Working a double crochet increase in the middle of a row.

Decreasing in single crochet

Working over the next two stitches, insert your hook into the next stitch, yarn over, and pull through the stitch (figure 1). (2 loops on hook)

Insert your hook in the next stitch, yarn over, and pull through the stitch. (3 loops on hook)

Yarn over (figure 2) and draw through all 3 loops (figure 3).

Decreasing in half double crochet

Working over the next two stitches, yarn over, insert your hook into the next stitch, yarn over, and pull through the stitch. (3 loops on hook)

Yarn over, insert your hook into the next stitch, yarn over, and pull through the stitch. (5 loops on hook)

Yarn over (figure 4) and draw through all 5 loops (figure 5).

Figure 1

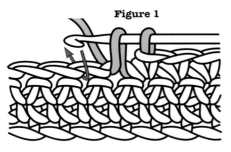

Beginning the second part of a single crochet decrease

Figure 4

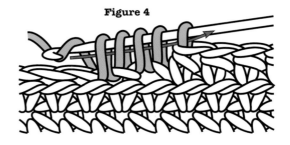

Figure 2

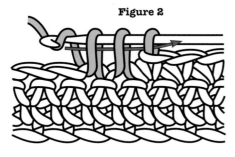

Finishing a single crochet decrease

Figure 5

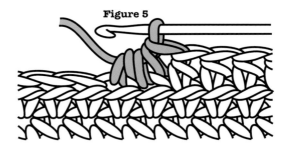

Figure 3

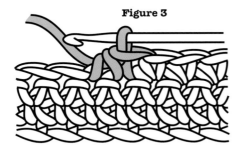

Decreasing in double crochet

Working over the next two stitches, yarn over, insert your hook into the next stitch, yarn over, and pull through the stitch. (3 loops on hook)

Yarn over and pull through the first two loops on your hook. (2 loops left on hook)

Yarn over (figure 6), insert your hook into the next stitch, yarn over, and pull through the stitch. (3 loops on hook)

Yarn over and pull through the first 2 loops on your hook. (3 loops left on hook)

Yarn over (figure 7) and draw through all 3 loops (figure 8).

Figure 7

Finishing double crochet decrease

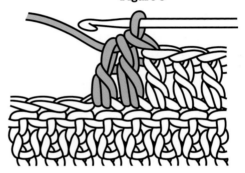

Figure 8

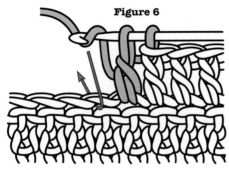

Figure 6

Beginning second part of double crochet decrease

Getting Your Gauge

For many years, I never gave any thought to gauge. It seemed confusing and time-consuming. I just made something and hoped it would come out right. After I made many adult tops that came out small enough for a baby, I realized that getting the right gauge *before* I began my project actually saves time and frustration.

Gauge is used to determine the finished size of your project. It is the number of stitches and the number of rows or rounds in 1 square inch of crocheted fabric. Every crochet pattern you'll run across is based on a particular gauge, and that information is usually found at the top of the pattern. In addition, every skein of yarn you buy will have a recommended gauge listed on its label. The gauge may look something like this:

14 sts = 4"

which means 14 stitches should measure 4 inches.

Why not just match the gauge on the pattern with the gauge on a yarn label?

That would seem to make sense, but the truth is that everyone crochets differently, even when using the same yarn and the same hook. For instance, my mother crochets much tighter than I do. The weather, your state of mind, or even your experience working with a particular type of yarn can affect your gauge. That's why it's always a good idea to crochet a gauge swatch before you start your project.

Get the yarn you intend to using and the size of hook suggested in your pattern and, using the project's stitch pattern, crochet a swatch that is at least 4 inches long and 4 inches wide. At that point, use a tape measure or knitter's window to measure your stitch gauge (how many stitches you are getting per 4 inches measuring across a row) and your row gauge (how many rows you are getting per 4 inches measuring up and down).

If you're getting more stitches or rows than is called for, switch to a hook that's one size bigger, crochet another swatch, and check your gauge again. Keep moving up a size until you get the gauge you're looking for. If you are getting fewer stitches or rows than is called for, switch to a hook that's one size smaller and check again.

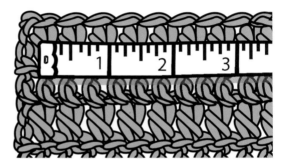

Measuring gauge with a tape measure.

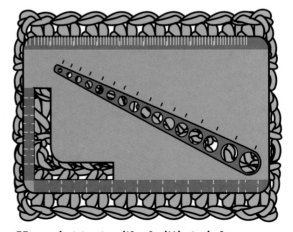

Measuring gauge with a knitting window.

Joining new yarn

To join yarn to crocheted work, insert your hook into the work as instructed in the pattern and pull up a loop of the new yarn, leaving a short tail for weaving in later on (figure 1). Work 1 chain, then continue to follow the directions.

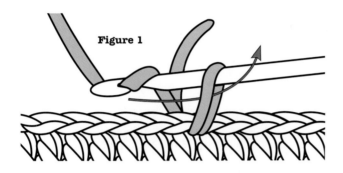

Figure 1

Changing Colors

When changing colors, don't finish the last stitch using the old color; leave two loops on the hook. Grab the new color with the hook (figure 2) and pull it through both loops to complete the stitch (figure 3). Continue working with the new color.

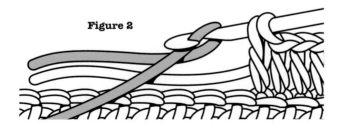

Figure 2

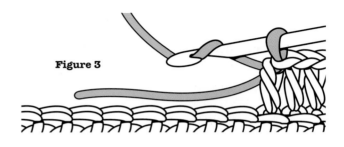

Figure 3

Fastening Off

When you are finished with a piece, clip the yarn about 5 inches away from the hook, then pull the thread through the last stitch (figure 4).

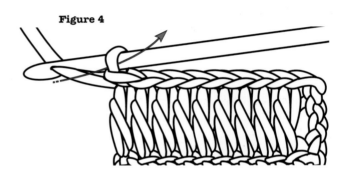

Figure 4

Finishing Touches

Once you've completed all or most all of your crocheting, you're in the home stretch. Here, we'll cover putting the pieces together, finishing techniques, and some fun add-ons you can use to customize your pieces.

Joining Pieces

Most of the projects in this book are created by crocheting separate panels, then joining them, either by sewing or crocheting them together. Usually, you will want to use the same color of yarn that was used in the pattern to do this, but you can also use a different color to add a little flavor, like a gold seam on a pair of jeans. Most seams will show up on the wrong side (the inside) of the item, making the edges invisible.

As you join the panels, make sure the stitches along each edge match up. If you're crocheting pieces together, use the same size hook that was used in the pattern, unless otherwise stated.

Backstitch seam

Match the sides and stitches of the panels together with the right or wrong sides facing each other. Using a weaving needle, work a backstitch seam along the edge.

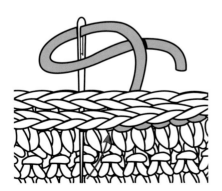

Joining two pieces with a backstitch seam

Slip-stitch seam

Match the sides and stitches of the panels together with the right or wrong sides facing each other. Work a row of slip stitches, going through both loops of each stitch on each piece. You can also join them together by crocheting through the back or front loops of each stitch. This will create a flatter seam.

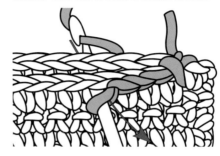

Joining two pieces using slip stitch

Single crochet seam

Match the sides and stitches of the panels together with the right or wrong sides facing each other. Work a row of single crochet, going through both loops of each stitch on each piece.

Joining two pieces with single crochet

Whipstitch seam

Match the sides and stitches of the panels together with the right or wrong sides facing each other. Insert the weaving needle from back to front. Bring the needle over the top, insert it into the next pair of stitches, and repeat to the end.

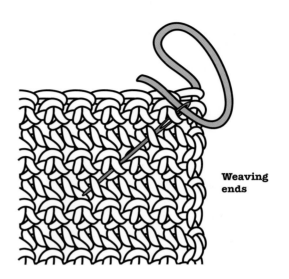

Weaving ends

Weaving in Yarn Ends

For a long time, when I finished a crocheted piece, I would just tie a knot in my yarn ends and call it a day. But my mother taught me how to weave in yarn ends, saying, "Presentation is half the sale." It really does make a difference—your item will look more finished, and weaving in ends will keep your work from coming apart. Securing the end of the yarn with fabric glue after you weave it in is optional. I started using fabric glue when I found that, after a few washes, the woven-in ends would start to peek out or the garment would begin to unravel. Adding a small dab of glue to the cut yarn ends after weaving them really keeps them in place.

Weaving as you go

You can weave in strands as you crochet along. This will save you time at the end.

Grab the loose yarn ends and work your stitch over them. If the stitch begins to look too bulky, grab fewer strands. My rule of thumb is two strands or less. If I am working with more that one color, I like to make sure that I position the color I am working with on the top.

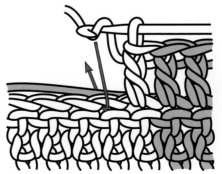

Yarn end being woven in as stitches are worked

Weaving In and Covering Elastic

For the majority of the patterns in this book, you can use round cord elastic and a weaving needle. Do not count the covering elastic as a row or round unless otherwise stated.

1. Weave the elastic through the last round of crochet. Read your pattern to see how tightly you should pull the elastic. When you've woven the elastic all the way through, you can adjust it by pulling it a bit tighter.

2. Tie a knot in the elastic and put a tiny bit of glue on the knot to hold it.

To cover the elastic, join the yarn in the last stitch you worked with the right side facing you. Continue working across your round by crocheting under and over the elastic. Chain 1, go through the next stitch, *[yarn over, pull through (2 loops on hook), go through the next stitch, yarn over, pull through (3 loops on hook), yarn over, pull through all 3 loops on hook, go through same stitch], repeat from * around, join.

Edging

When you want to join a panel, make a border, or smooth out an edge, you can work around your piece to make an edging. When you are working an edging within the pattern the number of stitches should correlate to the number in your next row or round. If you are working an edging at the end or egde of a piece, the number of stitches don't really matter as long as the piece looks even and nicely finished.

Picking-up stitches

You pick up stitches along the foundation chain (or upper horizontal edge). When working along the edge, insert the hook into both loops and work across. You should have the same number of stitches as you do in the previous row.

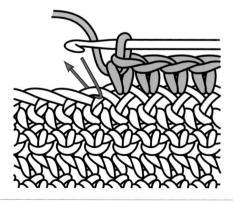

Picking up stitches along an upper horizontal edge

Row-end stitches

Row-end stitches are worked into the *side* of a stitch, rather than the stitch itself and appear at the ends of rows.

For example, if you are working in rows and you want to add a border around your piece of work, you would turn your work on its side, chain the indicated number of stitches, then insert your hook into the side of the stitch and crochet around the piece,

When working across row-end stitches, insert the hook where two stitches join together, at the base or the top of stitches, or both. You want to avoid gaps or holes across the edges. If the edge of your crocheted piece has end posts of double or triple crochet, you may have to work more than one stitch into each row-end stitch. If you're edging more than one panel or piece of the same size, try to end up with the same number of edging stitches on each one. Don't count the edging as a row unless otherwise stated.

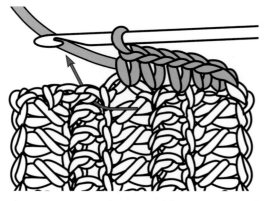

Single-crochet edging worked into row-end stitches

Turning corners

While working your edging, you will need to add multiple stitches to each corner so it lays flat and doesn't twist; see Increasing on page 31 for how to do this.

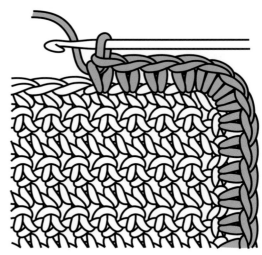

Corners

Blocking

Blocking is a method used to flatten corners, shape an item, or help something lay flat. You can do a wet block, steam block, heat block, or a starch block. In this book I have used heat blocking only for a few patterns, like the men's tie and Phat Laces.

To block, you need rust-proof pins, a towel or pillow case, and a steam iron.

Lay the item on the ironing board, cover it with the towel, and use the iron to steam, flatten, and shape the item.

A Little TLC

Whether an item needs to be hand washed or can be machine washed depends on the care instructions given on the yarn label, your resources, and whether the yarn has been preshrunk (some manufacturers will tell you that on the label, some won't). Before washing any piece, read the care instructions on the yarn's label (that means save the label!) and follow them.

Most cotton and acrylic yarns can be machine washed and dried. Many novelty yarns can safely be hand washed in cool to lukewarm water. Some yarn manufacturers will recommend dry-cleaning to protect themselves even though the finished garment really can be washed. The easiest way to tell for sure if a garment can be laundered is to make a swatch and test it (you could use your gauge swatch for this). Measure the swatch, then wash it, dry it, and remeasure it. This may sound like a lot of work, but I have learned from experience that this will save you a lot of headaches. After you have crocheted for a while and used different types of yarns, you will find a brand you like to work with and will become familiar with its cleaning requirements.

To machine wash

For machine washing, use cool to lukewarm water and set your machine to a gentle or delicate cycle. Turn the garment inside out and place it in a mesh laundry bag, then wash it.

To hand wash

For hand washing, place a gentle soap or detergent in a sink large enough to hold the garment. Add cool to lukewarm water and mix the soap into the water. Turn the garment inside out, place it in a mesh laundry bag, and set it in the water. Let it soak for about 20 minutes, swishing it around a couple of times. Drain the water and refill the sink with cool to lukewarm water to rinse. Place the garment in the water and gently swish it around a bit. Keep the water running and continue draining and refilling the sink until the water stays clear, then drain the sink. Let the garment drain thoroughly in the sink, then lightly press on it to release more water. To remove the remaining water, either roll it in a towel or put the item in a mesh laundry bag then put in the washer on the spin cycle.

To dry

You may lay your garment on a flat surface, like a counter or the top of the washer or dryer to let it dry. Garments made from cotton or acrylic yarn may be turned inside out, placed in a mesh laundry bag, and then tossed in the dryer on a low temperature setting for about 10 minutes just to remove excess water. After 10 minutes, remove it from the dryer and dry on a flat surface.

Dry-cleaning

I would recommend dry-cleaning any item made from a textured novelty yarn (unless otherwise noted on the yarn label). I've washed things made out of such yarns only to have them turn into fuzz balls. Again, read the yarn label. When in doubt, dry-clean!

Getting Rid of Fuzzies

Use an old electric razor or a fuzz remover (these can usually be found in a drugstore or discount store) to shave the fuzz from your garment.

Universal Care Symbols

Here are some of the symbols that are likely to show up on your yarn labels. It's a good idea to keep one yarn label for every project you make, stapling a piece of the yarn to it, for future laundering reference.

Symbol	Meaning	Symbol	Meaning
40° C 100° F	Hand Wash	Iron	Iron
40° C 100° F	Machine Wash in Lukewarm Water	Do Not Iron	Do Not Iron
Machine Dry	Machine Dry	A	Dry Clean
Do Not Machine Dry	Do Not Machine Dry	A	Do Not Dry Clean
Bleach	Bleach	P	Dry Clean using "P" Solvents
Do Not Bleach	Do Not Bleach		

The Patterns!

Biker Chain

This is a creative way to a little bling to your outfit. You can make it as long or as short as you'd like. Adding the swivel hooks on the end will allow you to clip the chain to your belt loops.

Materials needed:
120 yd lame metallic yarn
Size D/3 (3.25 mm) hook

Small weaving needle
2 swivel hooks or cobra key chains

Directions

Making the rings
Using 2 strands of yarn, ch 16.

1 sl st in 2nd ch from hook, 1 sl st in ea ch to end. Put one end of this strip through the first ring, then join the strip around the ring, then join the strip around the ring. Fasten off. Weave in the ends. Rep pattern until you have a total of 33 chains, or as many to get desired length.

Join the strip around the ring.

Attaching the swivel hooks
Using the weaving needle and a single strand of yarn, secure a swivel hook to each end of your chain by weaving the yarn through the loop of the swivel hook and the first or last chain.

Secure the swivel hook by weaving yarn through the hook and the first or last chain. Weave in any ends.

Chica

I got the inspiration for this pattern from one of my own belts. It can be worn low on the waist, right under the breast, or over a shirt or a coat.

Materials needed:
200 yd or two 2.5-oz (70.9-g) skeins of light or regular worsted-weight yarn

F/5 (4 mm) hook or size needed to obtain gauge

Weaving needle

Directions
Ch 136.

Row 1:	1 sc in 2nd ch from hook, 1 sc in ea ch to end. (135 sts)
Row 2:	Ch 1 (count as 1st st now and throughout), turn, 1 sc in 2nd st from hook, 1 sc in ea st until 2 sts remain (do not sc in last 2 sts). (133 sts)
Row 3:	Ch 1, turn, 1 sc in 2nd st from hook, 1 sc in ea st to end. (133 sts)
Row 4:	Rep row 2. (131 sts)
Row 3:	Rep row 3. (131 sts)
Row 6:	Rep row 2. (129 sts)
Row 7:	Rep row 3. (129 sts)
Row 8:	Ch 2, turn, 1 dc in 2nd st from hook, 1 dc in next 73 sts, 1 hdc in next 25 sts, 1 sc in next 27 sts (do not work the last 2 sts). (127 sts)
Row 9:	Ch 1, turn, 1 sc in 2nd st from hook, 1 sc in next 27 sts, 1 hdc in next 25 sts, 1 dc in ea st to end. (127 sts)
Row 10:	Ch 2, turn, 1 dc in 2nd st from hook, 1 dc in next 75 sts, 1 hdc in next 25 sts, 1 sc in next 25 sts. (2 sts will remain unworked in the row.) (127 sts) Fasten off.

With the RS facing you, join yarn in the right corner and work a sc edging around the panel, with 3 sc in ea corner.

Gauge:
13 dc = 4"

Join and fasten off.

Rep for a total of 2 panels.

Joining the panels
With RSs facing, match the corners of the panels. With the weaving needle, join the panels by sewing into the 1st two and last two sts. Go in and out of the sts three or four times to make sure the panels are securely attached.

Weave in all the ends.

Join the corners of the panels with a weaving needle. Weave in and out three or four times to secure.

Dashiki

This tunic style sweater is a twist on the traditional Afrikan top. Elastic is added under the breast for a snug fit.

Materials needed:

700 yd or two 8-oz (225-g) skeins of worsted-weight yarn in color A.

150 yd or one 8-oz (225-g) skein *each* of worsted-weight yarn in color B and color C

Size J/10 (6 mm) hook or size needed to obtain gauge

Weaving needle

Round cord elastic

Gauge:

7 dc(ch sp) = 4"

Sizes:

Small (Medium, Large, X-large)

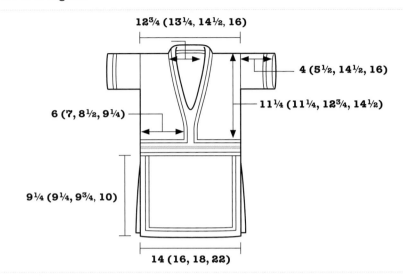

$12\frac{3}{4}$ ($13\frac{1}{4}$, $14\frac{1}{2}$, 16)

4 ($5\frac{1}{2}$, $14\frac{1}{2}$, 16)

$11\frac{1}{4}$ ($11\frac{1}{4}$, $12\frac{3}{4}$, $14\frac{1}{2}$)

6 (7, $8\frac{1}{2}$, $9\frac{1}{4}$)

$9\frac{1}{4}$ ($9\frac{1}{4}$, $9\frac{3}{4}$, 10)

14 (16, 18, 22)

Directions

Back panel

Using color A, ch 41(46,51,56), turn.

Row 1: 1 hdc in 2nd ch from hook, 1 hdc in ea ch to end. [40(45,50,55) sts]

Row 2: Ch 3 (count as 1st st now and throughout), turn, *(sk next st, 1 dc in next st, ch 1), rep from * to end but do not ch after last dc. [21(23,26,28) dc]

Rows 3–19(3–19,3–22,3–25): Ch 3, turn, *(sk next ch, 1 dc in next dc, ch 1), rep from *, to end but do not ch after last dc. [21(24,26,28) dc] Fasten off.

Front panels

Using color A, ch 21(23,26,28), turn.

Row 1: 1 hdc in 2nd ch from hook, 1 hdc in ea ch to end. [20(22,25,27) sts]

Row 2: Ch 3 (count as 1st st now and throughout), turn, *(sk next st, 1 dc in next st, ch 1), rep from* to end, but do not ch after last dc. [11(12,14,15) dc]

Rows 3–11: Ch 3, turn, *(sk next ch, 1 dc in next dc, ch 1), rep from *, to end but do not ch after last dc. [11(12,14,15) dc]

Rows 12–19(12–19,12–22,12–25): Ch 3, turn, *(sk next ch, 1 dc in next dc, ch 1), rep from * 7(8,10,11) more times but do not ch after last dc. [9(10,12,13) dc] Fasten off.

Rep for 2 panels

Joining the panels

Using color A, with RSs facing, join the side of the right front panel to the back panel with a whipstitch seam. Work the seam in ea dc and ch sp beginning at the bottom edge, working up the sides of rows 1–11. Fasten off.

Match the top corners of the right panel and the back panel and join with a whipstitch seam. Fasten off.

Rep for left panel (WS of front panel will be facing outside).

Match up the sides and the top, and join with a whipstitch seam.

Neck and panel edging

With the RSs facing, join color B at the bottom edge of the left panel. Work a sc edging around the bottom, inner edgings, and neck working 3 sc in ea corner and join.

Join color B at the bottom right corner.

Rnd 1:   Ch 1, 1 sc in ea st around entire top, working 3 sc in ea corner, join. [167(182,200,218) sts] Join color C.

Rnd 2:   Ch 1, 1 sc in ea st around, working 3 sc in ea corner, join. [172(188,206,224) sts] Fasten off.

Joining the two front panels

Turn the top inside out. Match the corners of the two front panels. Join color C at the bottom edge. Work a sl st seam in the 1st 8(10,12,14) sts. Fasten off.

Weave in yarn ends of sl st seam. Fasten off.

Match the ends of the two front panels and join with a slip-stitch seam.

Border

Turn the top RS out. Using the right side seam as a guide, join color C in the last row.

Rnd 1:   Ch 1, work 1 sc in ea st around, join. [87(90,103,216) sts] Weave elastic through rnd 1. Try on the top and see how you like the fit, adjusting the elastic the way you want it. Then cover the elastic (see page 38).

Rnd 2:   Ch 1, 1 sc in ea st around, join. [88(91,104,217) sts] Fasten off. Weave elastic through rnd 2, then cover using color B and join.

Join color C at the bottom edging, using the right seam as a guide.

Front panel of body

Sk 1st 2 sts and join color A in 3rd st.

Row 1:   Ch 3, *(sk next st, 1 dc in next st, ch 1), rep from * 20(22,24,32) times but do not ch after last dc. [22(24,26,34) dc]

Rows 2–13(2–13,2–14,2–15):
           Ch 3, turn, *(sk next st, 1 dc in next st, ch 1), rep from * to end but do not ch after last dc. [22(24,26,34) dc] Fasten off.

Back panel of body

Join color A in 3rd st from the last dc of row 1.

Row 1:   Ch 3, *(sk next st, 1 dc in next st, ch 1), rep from * 19(22,23,31) times but do not ch after last dc. [21(24,25,33) dc]

Rows 2–13(2–13,2–14,2–15):
           Ch 3, turn, *(sk next ch, 1 dc in next dc, ch 1), rep from * to end, but do not ch after last dc. [21(24,25,34) dc] Fasten off.

Front and back panel of body edging

Rnd 1:   With color A, work a sc edging around the front and back panels, working 3 sc in ea corner, join. [200(205,222,230) sts] Join color B.

Rnd 2:   Ch 1, 1 sc in ea st around, working 3 sc in ea corner, join. [208(213,230,238) sts] Join color C.

Rnd 3:   Ch 1, 1 sc in ea st around, working 3 sc in ea corner, join. [214(221,238,246) sts] Fasten off.

Joining the front and back panels of body

Turn top inside out and match up the right sides of the front and back panel trimming. Working from the top of the edging, join color C and work a sl st seam in the first 10 sts. Fasten off. Rep to join the other side.

Join the first 10 stitches of the front and back panels with a slip-stitch seam.

After the top has been put together, join color C to a corner, work an hdc edging around the front and back panels, working 3 hdc in each corner, and join. Fasten off.

Sleeves

With the garment RS out, join color A at the bottom seam of the arm hole. Work a hdc edging around the arm hole and join.

Rnds 1–5: Ch 2, 1 hdc in ea st around. [38(38,40,50) hdc] Join color B.

Rnds 6–7: Rep rnd 1. [38(38,40,50) hdc] Join color C.

Rnds 8–9: Rep rnd 1. [38(38,40,50) hdc] Fasten off. Rep for other sleeve. Weave in all the ends.

Tee La Rock

This mesh style tee fits best if made with acrylic yarn. Rock it with a tank top, T-shirt, or long-sleeved shirt underneath for different looks. The elastic around the neck gives it a real T-shirt fit.

Materials needed:

600(675,725,775,825) yd or two(two,three,three,three) 7-oz (198-g) skeins of worsted-weight yarn in color A

100 yd or one 7-oz (198-g) skein of worsted-weight yarn in color B

Size J/10 (6 mm) hook or size needed to obtain gauge

Weaving needle

Round cord elastic

Gauge:

8 dc (ch-2 sp) = 6"

Sizes:

Small (Medium, Large, X-large, XX-large)

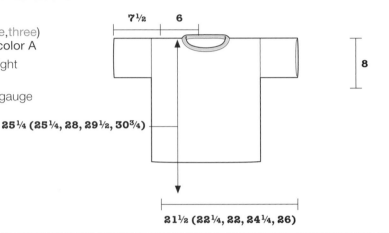

7½   6

8

25¼ (25¼, 28, 29½, 30¾)

21½ (22¼, 22, 24¼, 26)

Directions

Body

Using color A, ch 131(136, 141, 151, 156).
With WSs facing, join.

Rnd 1: Ch 2 (count as 1st st now and throughout), 1 hdc in 2nd ch from hook, 1 dc in ea ch around, join. [130(135,140,150,155) sts]

Rnd 2: Ch 4, *(sk next 2 sts, 1 dc in next st, ch 2), rep from * around, join. [43(45,47,51,52) dc]

Rnds 3–24(3–24,3–26,3–27,3–28):
Ch 4, *(sk next ch sp, 1 dc in next dc, ch 2), rep from * around, join. [43(45,47,51,52) dc]

Back

Row 1: Ch 4, *(sk next ch sp, 1 dc in next dc, ch 2, rep from * 18(18,21,22,23) times, but do not ch 2 after the last dc. [20(20,23,24,25) dc]

Rows 2–13(2–13,2–15,2–16,2–17):
Ch 4, turn, *(sk next ch sp, 1 dc in next dc, ch 2), rep from * 18(18,21,22,23) times, but do not ch 2 after the last dc. [20(20,23,24,25) dc] Fasten off.

Left front panel

With the front of the tee facing you, join color A in 2nd dc from end of row 1 of the back.

Rows 1–6(1–6,1–9,1–10,1–11):
Ch 4, turn, *(sk next ch sp, 1 dc in next dc, ch 2), rep from * 18(18,20,21,23) times, but do not ch 2 after the last dc. [20(20,22,23,25) dc]

Rows 7–8(7–8,10–11,11–12,12–13):
Ch 4, turn, *(sk next ch sp, 1 dc in next dc, ch 2), rep from * 6(6,7,9,10) times, but do not ch 2 after the last dc. [8(8,9,11,12) dc]

Tee La Rock... continued

Back

Join yarn in 2nd dc from back.

2 1

Join yarn in the 2nd double crochet from the back.

Rows 9–10(9–10,12–13,13–14,14–15):

    Ch 4, turn, *(sk next ch sp, 1 dc in next dc, ch 2), rep from * 5(5,6,8,9) times, but do not ch 2 after the last dc. [7(7,8,10,11) dc]

Rows 11–13(11–13,14–15,15–16,16–17):

    Ch 4, turn, *(sk next ch sp, 1 dc in next dc, ch 2), rep from * 4(4,5,7,8) times, but do not ch 2 after the last dc. [6(6,7,9,10) dc]

    Fasten off.

Right front panel

With RS facing you, join color A in the corner of row 6(6,9,10,11).

Rows 1–2: Ch 4, turn, *(sk next ch sp, 1 dc in next dc, ch 2), rep from * 6(6,7,9,10) times, but do not ch 2 after the last dc. [8(8,9,11,12) dc]

Rows 2–3: Ch 4, turn, *(sk next ch sp, 1 dc in next dc, ch 2), rep from * 5(5,6,8,9) times, but do not ch 2 after the last dc. [7(7,8,10,11) dc]

Rows 4–9: Ch 4, turn, *(sk next ch sp, 1 dc in next dc, ch 2), rep from * 4(4,5,7,8) times, but do not ch 2 after the last dc. [6(6,7,9,10) dc] Fasten off. Turn top inside out.

Join yarn in corner.

With the right side facing you, join color A in the corner of the noted row.

Match the edges and corners of the front and back panels and join with a sl st seam.

Neck

Turn top RS out, with the front of the top facing you, join color A at the inside left shoulder seam. Work a sc edging around the neck hole, join.

Join color B. Ch 1, 1 hdc in ea st around, join.

Weave elastic through last rnd. Pull the elastic snug but loose enough to get your head through, then cover the elastic (see page 38).

Sleeves

Join color A at the left arm seam.

Rnd 1:   Ch 2, work a sc edging around the arm hole, join.

Rnd 2:   Ch 4 (count as 1st st now and throughout, *(sk next 2 sts, ch 2, 1 dc in next st), rep from * around join. [21(21,22,23,23) dc]

Pull the elastic snug enough to fit around neck, but loose enough to get your head through.

Rnds 3–10:   Ch 4, *(sk next ch sp, ch 2, 1 dc in next dc), rep from * around join. [21(21,22,23,23) dc]

Rnds 11–12:   Ch 1, 1 hdc in ea dc and ch sp around, join. [42(42,44,46,46) sts] Fasten off.

Rep for second sleeve. Weave in all ends.

Juelz

These funky earrings can be made in a solid color or multiple colors in your choice of yarn—sport weight, worsted weight, textured, crochet thread, or craft cord.

Materials needed:

30 yd or one 3-oz (85-g) skein of crochet thread or sport-weight or nylon yarn (if using thread use 2 strands, if using sport weight or nylon, use 1 strand)

Size F/5 (3.75 mm) hook

4 cabone rings

Weaving needle

2 beads

2 fishhook wires

Directions

Making the rings

Ch 4, join to make a circle.

Rnd 1:   Ch 1, 11 hdc in circle, join.

Rnd 2:   Ch 1, 2 hdc in 2nd st from hook, 2 hdc in ea st to end. (22 sts)

Grab a ring and position the crocheted circle in the middle of it.

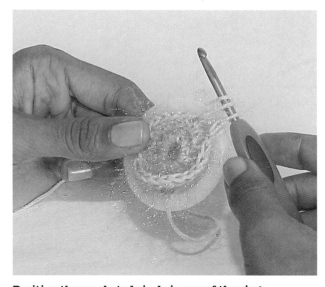

Position the crocheted circle in one of the rings and crochet over the ring.

Working over the ring

Rnd 3:   Ch 2, go through next st, pull the yarn through, and work a sc in ea st around crocheting over the ring, join.

Fasten off, leaving 2" of yarn.

Rep for a total of 4 rings.

Joining the rings

Join the round by threading the weaving needle with your 2" strand. Connect two of the rings by weaving through 1 st on each of the rings. Weave in and out of the stitch 3 or 4 times to make sure you have a secure connection.

Join two of the rings using a weaving needle and weaving in and out of both rings.

Adding the bead and hook

Add a bead at one end of the joined rings and secure with a knot.

Secure the ear hook with the needle and a strand of yarn and weave the end back through the bead and ring.

Cut and glue the yarn.

Rep for other two rings.

Weave in all the yarn ends.

Secure the bead and ear hook with a weaving needle.

Phat Laces

Pump up your new kicks with these creative shoestrings! Crochet thread makes shorter laces and are great for women and children's shoes. Using sport-weight yarn will make the laces longer, perfect for men's shoes and high tops!

120 yd or one 1.2-oz (35-g) skein crochet thread or sport-weight yarn each in colors A, B, and C (use 1 strand for yarn and 2 strands for thread)

Size D/3 (3.25 mm) hook or size needed to obtain gauge

Foil tape

Fabric glue

Gauge:
Crochet thread, 18 sc = 4"

Sport-weight yarn, 17 sc = 4"

Measurements:
Crochet thread: lace should measure 50" with a slight stretch

Sport-weight yarn: lace should measure 80" with a slight stretch

Directions
Using color A (and double strands if using crochet thread), ch 216.

Row 1:   1 sl st in 2nd ch from hook, 1 sl st in next 3 chs, 1 sc in next 207 chs, 1 sl st in last 4 chs. (215 sts) Join color B.

Row 2:   Ch 1 (count as 1st st now and throughout), turn, 1 sl st in next 4 sts, 1 sc in next 207 sts, 1 sl st in last 4 sts. (216 sts) Join color C.

Row 3:   Ch 1, turn, 1 sl st in next 4 sts, 1 sc in next 207 sts, 1 sl st in last 4 sts. (216 sts)

Rep for second lace.

Ends
Match up the ends of three 10" loops of any of the colors of yarn. (If you are using double strands also use double strands for this.)

Fasten the loops to one of the shoelaces.

Insert the crochet hook into the end of the lace, fold the strips in half, and pull through, then yo and pull all the strands through the loop on the hook to make a slip knot.

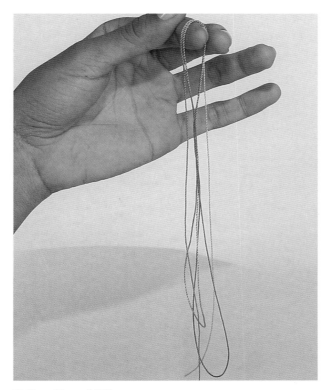

Pull up three 10" loops.

Pull the loops through the tips of the lace. Yarn over, then pull all the strands through the loop on the hook, making a slip knot.

Cut the bottom of the loops and, using two strands as one, braid the lengths. Fasten off.

Lay a 1" piece of tape on the table.

Glue one side of the braid and lay it on the side of the tape.

Add glue to the other side of the braid. Wrap the tape around the braid 2 times very tightly.

Lay the glued side of the braid on the tape.

Wrap the tape around the braid twice, very tightly.

Trim the yarn. Glue the tip of the cut yarn to make the tip sturdier.

Rep for second lace.

Shawty

This pattern is a twist on a shrug. It can be worn over a T-shirt, tank top, tube or even a dress in any of these styles.

Materials needed:

350(415,480) yd or three(four,four) 2.5-oz (70.9-g) skeins of worsted-weight yarn in color A

100 yd or one 2.5-oz (70.9-g) skein of worsted-weight yarn in color B

Size J/10 (6 mm) hook or size needed to obtain gauge

Weaving needle

Round cord elastic

Gauge:

10 hdc = 4"

Sizes:

Small (Medium, Large)

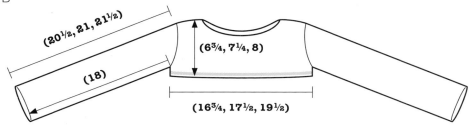

Directions

Bottom

Using color A, ch 91(101,111), join with WSs facing.

Rnd 1:   Ch 1, 1 hdc in ea ch around, join. [90(100,110) sts]

Rnd 2:   (Count as 1st st now and throughout) 1 hdc in 2nd st from hook, ch 1, 1 hdc in ea st around, join. [90(100,110) sts]

Do not fasten off. Now you will begin the front of the top.

Front

Row 1:   Ch 1, 1 hdc in 2nd st from hook, 1 hdc in next 41(46,51) sts. [43(48,53) sts]

You will begin to decrease in the next 2 rows by skipping last 2 sts.

Row 2:   Ch 1 (count as 1st st now and throughout),

turn, 1 hdc in 2nd st from hook, 1 hdc in next 39(44,49) sts. [41(46,51) sts]

Row 3:   Ch 1, turn, 1 hdc in 2nd st from hook, 1 hdc in next 37(42,47) sts. [39(44,49) sts]

Row 4:   Ch 1, turn, 1 hdc in 2nd st from hook, 1 hdc in next 31(36,41) sts, work 2 dec over the next 4 sts. [35(40,45) sts]

Row 5:   Ch 1, turn, 1 hdc in 2nd st from hook, 1 hdc in next 27(34,37) sts, work 2 dec over the last 4 sts. [31(36,41) sts]

Do not fasten off. For small and medium, skip to side 1.

Continue for Large.

Row 6:   Ch 1, turn, 1 hdc in 2nd st from hook, 1 hdc in ea st to end. 31(36,41) sts]

Side 1

Continue working to make strap.

Row 1: Ch 1, turn, 1 hdc 1st st from hook, 1 hdc in next 6 sts. (7, 8 sts)

Rows 2-8(2-9, 2-10):
Ch 1, turn, 1 hdc in 2nd st from hook, 1 hdc in 6 (7,8) sts. (8,9,10 sts)
Fasten off.

Side 2

With front of top facing you, join color A in the right corner.

Rows 1–8(1–9,1–10):
Ch 1, turn, 1 hdc in next 8 sts. (8 sts)
Fasten off.

Back

With back of the top facing you, join color A in the 3rd st from row 1 of the front.

Row 1: Ch 1, 1 hdc in first st from hook, 1 hdc in next 41(46,51) sts. [43(48,53)sts]

Row 2: Ch 1, turn, 1 hdc in 2nd st from hook, 1 hdc in next 39(44,49) sts. [41(46,51) sts]

Row 3: Ch 1, turn, 1 hdc in 2nd st from hook, 1 hdc in next 37(42,47) sts. [39(44,49) sts]

Rows 4–7: Ch 1, turn, 1 hdc in 2nd st from hook, 1 hdc in next 35(40,45) sts. [37(42,47) sts]

Do not fasten off.

Side 1

Continue working to make side 1.

Row 1: Ch 1, turn, 1 hdc in 1st st from hook, 1 hdc in next 6 (7,8) sts. (8,9,10 sts)

Rows 2-8(2-9, 2-10):
Ch 1, turn, 1 hdc in 2nd st from hook, 1 hdc in next 6 (7,8) sts. (8,9,10 sts)

Fasten off.

Side 2

With the back of the top facing you for small and large, join color A in the back right corner. For medium with front facing, join color A in the back right corner.

Join yarn in the back right corner.

Row 1:   Ch 1, turn, hdc in 1st st from hook, 1 hdc in next 6(7,8) sts. (8,9,10 sts)

Turn top inside out and join front and back sides with a sl st seam. Fasten off.

Rows 2-8(2-9, 2-10):
        Ch 1, turn, 1 hdc in 2nd st from hook, 1 hdc 1 next 6(7,8) sts. (8,9,10 sts)

Neck

Turn top RS out, join color A at the inside shoulder seam, work a sc edging around the neck, join.

Weave elastic through the edging; then cover the elastic (see page 38). Fasten off.

Finishing

Weave elastic through the bottom edging and cover with color A. Fasten off.

Sleeves

Join color A at the arm seam, work a sc edging around, join.

Rnds 1–3:   Ch 1, 1 hdc in ea st around, join. [36(39,45) sts]

Rnd 4:   Ch 1, *(1 hdc in next 3 sts, dec over next 2 sts), rep from * around, join. [31(32,37) sts]

Rnds 5–34:   Rep rnd 1 but don't join at end of each rnd, instead, work in continuous rnds through rnd 34, then join with a slip st. [31(32,37) sts] Join color B.

Rnd 35:   Rep rnd 1. [31(32,37) sts] Join color A.

Rnd 36:   Rep rnd 1. [31(32,37) sts] Join color B.

Rnd 37:   Rep rnd 1. [31(32,37) sts] Join color A.

Rnds 38–39:   Rep rnd 1. [31(32,37) sts] Join color B.

Rnd 40:   Rep rnd 1. [31(32,37) sts] Join color A.

Rnd 41:   Rep rnd 1. [31(32,37) sts] Join color B.

Rnd 42:   Rep rnd 1. [31(32,37) sts] Join color A.

Rnds 43–45 (43–47, 43–49):
        Rep rnd 5.
        Join after last rnd.

Continue in this manner adding rows and alternating colors as needed for longer arms. Fasten off.

Rep for other sleeve. Weave in all the ends.

Shorties

These fingerless gloves are great for a cool fall or spring day.
Using a sparkly yarn will give them a look that can be worn on a night out.

Materials needed:

200 yd or one 1.75-oz (50-g) skein of light or regular worsted-weight yarn

Size H/8 (5 mm) hook or size needed to obtain gauge

Weaving needle

Round cord elastic

Gauge:

12 hdc = 4"

Sizes:

Small/Medium (Large/X-large)

Directions

Ribbing

Ch 11

Row 1:   1 sc in ea ch to end. (10 sts)

Rows 2–22(2–26):
Ch 1, turn (work in back loops only now and throughout ribbing), 1 sc in 2nd st from hook, 1 sc in ea st to end. (10 sts)

With RSs facing, join two shorter sides with a sl st seam.

Turn ribbing to RS, ch 1, work a sc edging around, join.

Weave elastic through the edging and cover (see page 38). Fasten off.

Work a sc edging around other side of the ribbing.

Weave elastic through the edging and cover.

Do not fasten off. Now you will begin the hand.

Hand

Rnd 1:   Ch 1, 1 hdc in 2nd st from hook, 1 hdc in ea st around, do not join. [26(28) sts]

Rnds 2–8(2–9):
Ch 1, turn, 1 hdc in 2nd st from hook, 1 hdc in ea st around, do not join. [26(28) sts] Fasten off.

Turn the glove inside out and join only the corners with a weaving needle.

Turn the glove inside out, match the left corners, then join only the corners with a weaving needle.

Thumb

Join yarn at the seam.

Rnd 1:   Ch 1, work a hdc edging around hole. (17 sts)

Rnd 2:   Ch 1, *(1 hdc in next 2 sts, dec over next 2 sts), rep from * around, join. (14 sts)

Rnd 3:   Rep rnd 2. (7 sts) Fasten off.

Weave in all ends.

Rep for second glove.

Stay Up

This unisex belt can be jazzed up by using different a colored and/or sized belt buckle, or you can even add the N'Digi pouch to it.

Materials needed:

150 yd or one 7-oz (200-g) skein of nylon yarn or worsted-weight yarn

Size F/5 (4 mm) hook or size needed to obtain gauge

Weaving needle

Belt buckle

Gauge:

16 sc = 4"

Sizes:

Small (Medium, Large, X-large)

Measurements:

38" (42", 48", 55")

Directions

Ch 141(161,171,201)

Row 1:   1 sc in 2nd ch from hook, 1 sc in ea ch to end. [140(160,170,200) sts]

Rows 2–3: Ch 1 (count as 1st st now and throughout), turn, 1 sc in 2nd st from hook, 1 sc in ea st to end. [140(160,170,200) sts]

Note: You will be making belt holes in row 4.

Row 4:   Ch 1, 1 sc in 2nd st from hook, 1 sc in ea st until you get to the 15th st, *(ch 2, sk next 2 sts, 1 sc in next 2 sts), rep from * 7 times, 1 sc in ea st to end. 101(140,153,182 sc]

The finished belt holes.

Row 3:   Ch 1, turn, 1 sc in 2nd st from hook, 1 sc in ea st and 2 sc in ea ch-2 sp to end. [113(158,170,198) sts]

Rows 6–7: Rep row 1. [113(158,170,198) sts] Fasten off.

Belt loop

Ch 20

Row 1:   1 sc in 2nd ch from hook, 1 sc in ea ch to end. (19 sts)

Row 2:   Ch 1, 1 sc in 2nd st from hook, 1 sc in ea st to end. (19 sts)

Fasten off, leaving a 4" strand of yarn to join.

Join ends with a weaving needle to form a ring.

Putting on the belt buckle

Slide the belt loop on the end of the belt that does not have the holes.

Measure 2½" from the edge. Insert the pin of the buckle there, positioning it vertically in the middle of the belt. Fold the short end of the belt over the buckle, connecting it to the belt.

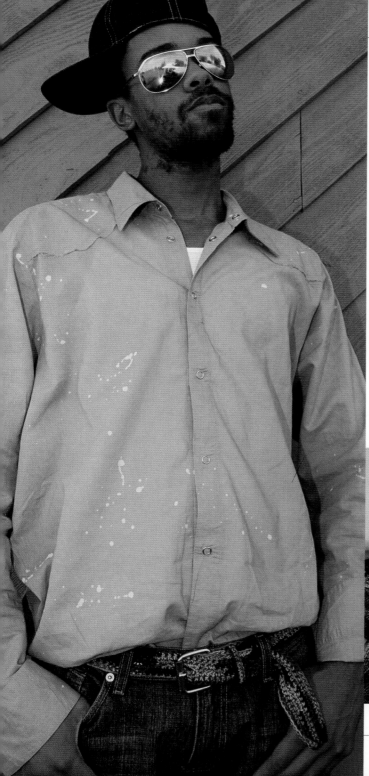

Position the belt loop in between the buckle and the end of the belt. Turn the belt over and secure about ½" of the folded end of the belt to the long part of the belt using a weaving needle.

Weave in all the ends.

After positioning the end of the belt over the buckle, secure the buckle by securing the folded end to the long part of the belt.

Sporties

I have always had a difficult time following sock patterns, and I knew there must be an easier way to make socks. So I came up with using two tubes, one for the leg and one for the foot, then connecting them before making the heel and toes. I hope you enjoy these as much as I do!

Materials needed:
350 yd or two 1.75-oz (50-g) skeins of sport- or sock-weight yarn for color A

50 yd or one 1.75-oz (50-g) skein of sport- or sock-weight yarn for color B

Size F/3 (3.25 mm) hook or size needed to obtain gauge

Weaving needle

Round cord elastic

Gauge:
20 hdc = 4"

Sizes:
Women's 6–8 (9–11)

Directions

Ribbing

With color A, ch 11.

Row 1:   1 hdc in 2nd ch from hook, 1 hdc in ea ch to end. (10 sts)

Rows 2–38(2–45):
           Ch 1, turn (work in back loops only now and throughout ribbing), 1 hdc in 2nd st from hook, 1 hdc in ea st around. (10 sts)

With RSs facing, join the two shorter sides with a sl st seam.

Turn the ribbing to RS, ch 1, work a sc edging around, join.

Weave elastic through the edging and cover (see page 38). Fasten off.

Work a sc edging around other side of the ribbing and join.

Weave elastic through the edging and cover.

Do not fasten off. Now begin the leg.

Leg
Rnd 1:   Ch 1, 1 hdc in 2nd st from hook and in ea st around, join. [56(61) sts] Join color B.

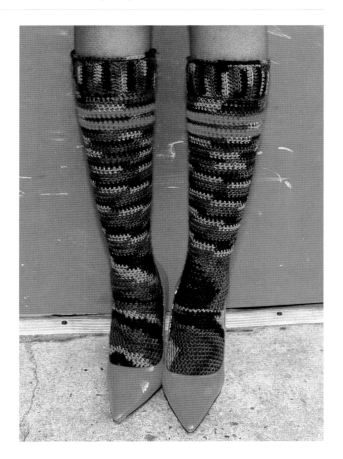

Rnd 2:	Rep rnd 1. [56(61) sts] Join color A
Rnd 3:	Rep rnd 1. [56(61) sts] Join color B.
Rnd 4:	Rep rnd 1. [56(61) sts] Join color A.
Rnds 5–10(5–12):	Ch 1, 1 hdc in 2nd st from hook, 1 hdc in ea st around. Do not join, work in continuous rnds through last rnd, join after last rnd. [56(61) sts]
Rnd 11(13):	Ch 1, *(1 hdc in next 3 sts, dec over next 2 sts), rep from * around, join. [45(49) sts]
Rnds 12–30(14–32):	Rep rnd 5. [45(49) sts]
Rnd 31(33):	Ch 1, *(1 hdc in next 9 sts, dec over next 2 sts), rep from * around, join. [41(44) sts]
Rnds 32–40(34–42):	Rep rnd 5. [41(44) sts]

At this point, you can add more hdc rows if you need to make the legs longer. Fasten off.

Foot tube

With color A, ch 40(46), join to form a ring.

Rnd 1:	Ch 1, 1 hdc in 2nd ch from hook, 1 hdc in ea ch around, join. [39(45) sts]
Rnds 2–20(2–22):	Ch 1, 1 hdc in 2nd ch from hook, 1 hdc in ea ch around. Do not join, work in continuous rnds through last rnd, join after last rnd. [39(45) sts]
Rnd 21(23):	Ch 1, *(1 sc in next 2 sts, dec over next 2 sts), rep from * around, join. [23(34) sts]

Join the ends of the leg and the foot tube with a slip-stitch seam.

Rnds 22–30(24–32):
Ch 1, 1 sc in 2nd st from hook, 1 sc in ea st around. Join. [23(34) sts]

Rnd 31(33):
Rep rnd 21(23). [19(25) sts]

Rnd 32(34):
Rep rnd 22(24). [19(25) sts]

Rnd 33(35):
Rep rnd 21(23). [14(20) sts]

Rnd 34(36):
Rep rnd 22(24). [14(20) sts] Fasten off.

Joining the tube and leg

With the RSs facing, match the end of the leg and the end of the foot tube and, using color A, join them with a sl st seam in the next 20 sts.

Do not fasten off. Now begin to close the heel.

Making the heel

Rnds 1–4: Ch 1, 1 hdc in ea st around, join [37(42) sts]

Rnd 5: Ch 1, *(1 hdc in next 3 sts, dec over next 2 sts), rep from * around, join. [29(32) sts]

Rnd 6: Ch 1, 1 hdc in ea st around, join. [32(37) sts]

Rnd 7: Rep rnd 5. [23(27) sts]

Rnd 8: Rep rnd 5. [19(20) sts] Continue for size 9–11.

Rnd 9: Rep rnd 5. (16 sts)

Turn the sock inside out and join with a sl st seam.

Fasten off. Weave in all ends.

Rep for second sock.

Holla Back

This design was inspired by a backless T-shirt that was given to me by a friend. It's warm, cute, and sexy.

Materials needed:

350(450,525,650) yd or one (two,two,two) 7-oz (198-g) skeins of worsted-weight yarn in color A

100(120,135,150) yd or one 7-oz (198-g) skein *each* of worsted-weight yarn in colors B, C, and D

Size J/10 (6 mm) hook or size needed to obtain gauge

Weaving needle

Round cord elastic

Gauge:

11 dc = 4"

Sizes:

Small (Medium, Large, X-large)

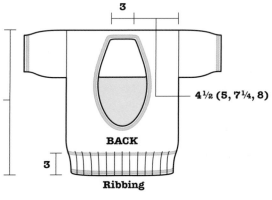

Ribbing

Using color A, ch 11.

Row 1: 1 sc in 2nd ch from hook, 1 sc in ea ch to end. (10 sts)

Rows 2–80(2–90,2–104,2–115): Ch 1 (count as 1 st now and throughout ribbing), turn, (working in back loops only now and throughout ribbing) 1 sc in ea st to end. (10 sts)

With RSs facing, join 2 smaller sides with a sl st seam. Do not fasten off.

Join the ribbing with a slip-stitch seam.

Ch 1, then work a sc edging along one of the long sides of the ribbing and join.

Weave the elastic through the edging and cover (see page 38). Fasten off.

Join color A to the other side of the ribbing, work a sc edging around, and join.

Weave elastic through the edging and cover. Do not fasten off. Now you'll begin the body.

Work a single crochet edging around the ribbing on both sides.

Body

Rnd 1(1–2,1–3,1–4):
Ch 2, 1 dc in 1st st from hook, 1 dc in ea st around, join. [83(93,105,116) sts]
Join color B.

Rnd 2(3,4,5):
Rep rnd 1. [83(93,105,116) sts]
Join color C.

Rnd 3(4,5,6):
Rep rnd 1. [83(93,105,116) sts]
Join color D.

Rnd 4(5,6,7):
Rep rnd 1. [83(93,105,116) sts]
Join color A.

Rnd 5(6,7,8):
Rep rnd 1. [83(93,105,116) sts]
Join color B.

Rnd 6(7,8,9):
Rep rnd 1. [83(93,105,116) sts]
Do not fasten off. Now you'll begin the back.

Back, side 1

Join color C.

Row 1:
Ch 2 (count as 1st st now and throughout), 1 dc in 1st st from hook, 1 dc in next 17(19,23,25 sts). [19(21,25,27) sts] Join color D.

Row 2:
Ch 2, turn, 1 dc in 2nd st from hook, 1 dc in ea ch to end. [19(21,25,27) sts]

At this point, you will begin decreasing by not working into the last st of each row. Join color A.

Row 3:
Ch 2, turn, 1 dc in 2nd st from hook, 1 dc in next 16(18,22,24) sts. [18(20,24,26) sts] Join color B.

Row 4:
Ch 2, turn, 1 dc in 2nd st from hook, 1 dc in next 15(17,21,23) sts. [17(19,23,25) sts] Join color C.

Row 5:
Ch 2, turn, 1 dc in 2nd st from hook, 1 dc in next 14(16,20,22) sts. [16(18,22,24) sts] Join color D.

Row 6:
Ch 2, turn, 1 dc in 2nd st from hook, 1 dc in next 13(15,19,21) sts. [15(17,21,23) sts] Join color A.

Row 7:
Ch 2, turn, 1 dc in 2nd st from hook, 1 dc in next 12(14,18,20) sts. [14(16,20,22) sts] Join color B.

Row 8:
Ch 2, turn, 1 dc in 2nd st from hook, 1 dc in next 11(13,17,19) sts. [13(15,19,21) sts] Join color C.

Row 9:	Ch 2, turn, 1 dc in 2nd st from hook, 1 dc in next 10(12,16,18) sts. [12(14,18,20) sts] Join color D.
Row 10:	Ch 2, turn, 1 dc in 2nd st from hook, 1 dc in next 9(11,15,17) sts. [11(13,17,19) sts] Join color A.
Row 11:	Ch 2, turn, 1 dc in 2nd st from hook, 1 dc in next 9(10,14,16) sts. [10(12,16,18) sts]
Rows 12–20:	Ch 2, turn, 1 dc in 2nd st from hook, 1 dc in next 8(9,13,15) sts. [9(11,15,17) sts]
Row 21:	Ch 2, 1 dc in 1st st from hook, 1 dc in ea st to end. [10(12,16,18) sts]
Row 22:	Rep row 21. [11(13,17,19) sts]
Row 23:	Rep row 21. [12(14,18,20) sts]
Row 24:	Rep row 21. [13(15,19,21) sts] Fasten off.

Back, side 2

With the back facing you, join color C in the 3rd st from the 1st row of side 1.

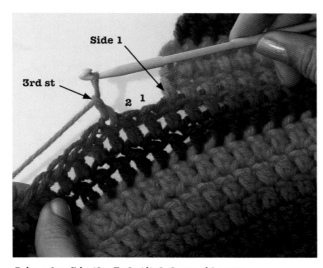

Join color C in the 3rd stitch from side one.

Rep instructions for side 1. Fasten off.

With the back facing you, join color A in the left corner of side 1, ch 10, and join to the corner of side 2.

Chain 10 and join to the corner of side two.

Ch 1 and work a sc edging in ch sts around the opening you've just made and join. Do not fasten off.

Weave elastic through the edging and cover (see page 38). Fasten off.

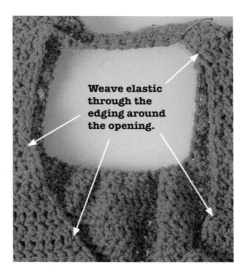

Weave elastic through the edging around the opening.

Front

With the front facing you and the garment RS out, join color C on the right side, in the st next to row 1 of the back.

Note: As you are changing colors, do not weave your ends as you go. Leave a 4" strand of yarn when ending and adding colors to join the front and back later on.

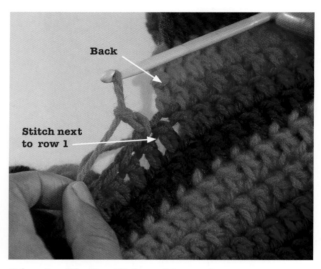

Back

Stitch next to row 1

Join color C in the stitch next to row 1.

Row 1:   Ch 2 (count as 1st st now and throughout), 1 dc in 1st st from hook, 1 dc in next 41(46,50,59) sts. [43(48,52,61) sts] Join color D.

Row 2:   Ch 2, turn, 1 dc in 2nd st from hook, 1 dc in ea st to end. [43(48,52,61) sts] Join color A.

Row 3:   Rep row 2. [43(48,52,61) sts] Join color B.

Row 4:   Rep row 2. [43(48,52,61) sts] Join color C.

Row 5:   Rep row 2. [43(48,52,61) sts] Join color D.

Row 6:   Rep row 2. [43(48,52,61) sts]
           Join color A.

Row 7:   Rep row 2. [43(48,52,61) sts]
           Join color B.

Row 8:   Rep row 2. [43(48,52,61) sts]
           Join color C.

Row 9:   Rep row 2. [43(48,52,61) sts]
           Join color D.

Row 10:   Rep row 2. [43(48,52,61) sts]
           Join color A.

Row 11:   Rep row 2. [43(48,52,61) sts] Do not fasten
           off. Now begin strap 1 of the front.

Strap 1

Row 1:   Ch 2 (count as 1st st now and throughout),
           1 dc in 2nd st from hook, 1 dc in next
           5(6,8,10) sts. [7(8,10,12) sts] Join color B.

Row 2:   Rep row 1. [7(8,10,12) sts]
           Join color A.

Rows   Rep row 1. [7(8,10,12) sts]
3-13:   Fasten off.

Strap 2

With the back of the top facing you, join color A in the
front right corner.

Rep instructions for strap 1. Do not fasten off.

Joining the front and back

Turn the tee inside out, match the front and back corners
together, and join the top sides (straps) with a sl st seam.

Turn the tee to the side and join the front and back side
edges of with a whipstitch seam through row 12, using the
4" strands you left when ending and adding colors for the
front. Fasten off.

**Match the corners and join the top straps with
a slip-stitch seam.**

**Join the front and back side edges with a whipstitch
seam.**

Neck

Join color A at an inside shoulder seam and work a sc edging around the neck hole. Join. Fasten off.

Weave elastic through the edging tight enough so that it puckers a little in the front.

Cover the elastic using color A (see page 38), then work a sl st in ea st around, and join. Fasten off.

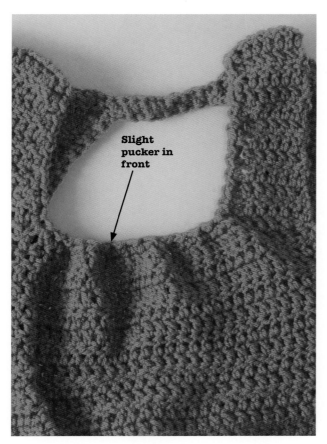

Pull the elastic tight enough so that you get a slight pucker in the front.

Slight pucker in front

Sleeves

Join color A at the underarm seam, work a sc edging around, and join.

Rnd 1:   Ch 2 (count as 1st st now and throughout), 1 dc in 1st st and in ea st around, join. [43(43,45,51) sts]

Rnd 2:   Ch 2, (working in back loops in this row only) 1 dc in ea st around, join. [43(43,45,51) sts]

Rnds 3–9: Ch 2, 1 dc in ea st around. Do not join; continue to work in continuous rnds through rnd 9, then join at the end of rnd 9.

Weave elastic through last rnd, pulling it until the sleeve fits snug around your arm, then cover. Fasten off.

Rep to make second sleeve. Weave in all the ends.

Boss Up

The right tie can add flair to any outfit. And women, don't let the men have all the fun—
try this yourself for a completely different look.

Materials needed:

120 yd or one 1.75-oz (50-g) skein of sock-weight or
sport-weight yarn

D/3 (3.25 mm) hook

Small weaving needle

Stitch markers

Directions

Ch 4.

Row 1:	1 sc in 2nd ch from hook, ch 1, sk next ch, 1 sc in last ch. (2 sc) **Note:** Use stitch markers to keep track of the rows.
Rows 2–60:	Ch 2 (count as 1st st now and throughout), turn, 1 sc in next ch sp, ch 1, sk next sc, 1 sc in last st. (3 sc)
Row 61:	Ch 2, turn, 1 sc in 1st ch sp, ch 1, 1 sc in same ch sp, ch 1 sk next sc, 1 sc in last st. (4 sc)
Rows 62–150:	Ch 2, turn, *(1 sc in next ch sp, ch 1), rep from * once, sk next sc, 1 sc in last st. (4 sc)
Row 151:	Ch 2, turn, 1 sc in 1st ch sp, *(ch 1, 1 sc in next ch sp), rep from * once, sk next sc, 1 sc in last st. (5 sc)
Rows 152–175:	Ch 2, turn, *(1 sc in next ch sp, ch 1), rep from * twice, sk next sc, 1 sc in last st. (5 sc)
Row 176:	Ch 2, turn, 1 sc in 1st ch sp, *(ch 1, 1 sc in next ch sp), rep from * twice, sk next sc, 1 sc in last st. (6 sc)
Rows 177–183:	Ch 2, turn, *(1 sc in next ch sp, ch 1), rep from * 3 times, sk next sc, 1 sc in last st. (6 sc)
Row 184:	Ch 2, turn, *(1 sc in next ch sp, ch 1), rep from * 4 times, sk next sc, 1 sc in last st. (7 sc)

Rows 185–200:	Ch 2, turn, *(1 sc in next ch sp, ch 1), rep from * 4 times, sk next sc, 1 sc in last st. (7 sc)
Row 201:	Ch 2, turn, *(1 sc in next ch sp, ch 1), rep from * 5 times, sk next sc, 1 sc in last st. (8 sc)
Rows 202–220:	Ch 2, turn, *(1 sc in next ch sp, ch 1), rep from * 5 times, sk next sc, 1 sc in last st. (8 sc)
Row 221:	Ch 2, turn, *(1 sc in next ch sp, ch 1), rep from * 3 times, * (1 sc in next ch sp, ch 1) repeat from * twice, sk next sc, 1 sc in last st. (9 sc)
Rows 222–235:	Ch 2, turn, *(1 sc in next ch sp, ch 1), rep from * 6 times, sk next sc, 1 sc in last st. (9 sc)
Row 236:	Ch 2, turn, *(1 sc in next ch sp, ch 1), rep from * 4 times, * (1 sc in next ch sp, ch 1) repeat from * twice, sk next sc, 1 sc in last st. (10 sc)
Rows 237–270:	Ch 2, turn, *(1 sc in next ch sp, ch 1), rep from * 7 times, sk next sc, 1 sc in last st. (10 sc)
Row 271:	Ch 2, turn, *(1 sc in next ch sp, ch 1), rep from * 5 times, * (1 sc in next ch sp, ch 1) repeat from * twice, sk next sc, 1 sc in last st. (11 sc)
Rows 272–300:	Ch 2, turn, *(1 sc in next ch sp, ch 1), rep from * 8 times, sk next sc, 1 sc in last st. (11 sc) From here, you will begin to decrease and make the point of the tie.

Boss Up... continued

Row 301: Ch 1, turn, sk 1st ch, *(1 sc in next ch sp, ch 1), rep from * 7 times, sk next sc, 1 sc in last st. (10 sc)

Row 302: Ch 1, turn, sk 1st ch, *(1 sc in next ch sp, ch 1, rep from * 6 times, sk next sc, 1 sc in last st. (9 sc)

Row 303: Ch 1, turn, sk 1st ch, *(1 sc in next ch sp, ch 1), rep from * 5 times, sk next sc, 1 sc in last st. (8 sc)

Row 304: Ch 1, turn, sk 1st ch, *(1 sc in next ch sp, ch 1), rep from * 4 times, sk next sc, 1 sc in last st. (7 sc)

Row 305: Ch 1, turn, sk 1st ch, *(1 sc in next ch sp, ch 1), rep from * 3 times, sk next sc, 1 sc in last st. (6 sc)

Row 306: Ch 1, turn, sk 1st ch, *(1 sc in next ch sp, ch 1), rep from * twice, sk next sc, 1 sc in last st. (5 sc)

Row 307: Ch 1, turn, sk 1st ch, *(1 sc in next ch sp, ch 1), rep from * once, sk next sc, 1 sc in last st. (4 sc)

Row 308: Ch 1, turn, sk 1st ch, 1 sc in next ch sp, ch 1), sk next sc, 1 sc in last st. (3 sc)

Row 309: Ch 1, turn, sk 1st ch and sc, 1 sc in last st. (2 sc) Do not fasten off.

Finishing

Ch 1 and work a sc edging around entire tie, working 3 sc in the tip (between the 2 sc of row 309), 2 sc at row 301 and 2 sc in top (smaller) corners, join.

Rnd 1: Ch 1, work 1 sc in ea st around, working 3 sc in the sc in the center of the tip and 2 sc in ea corner, join. (591 sc)

Rnd 2: Ch 1, work 1 sc in ea st around, working 3 sc in the sc in the center of the tip and 2 sc in ea corner, join. (597 sc) Fasten off. Weave in all the ends. Use steam blocking (see page 39) to flatten the corners.

Steppin Out

This belt is quick, simple, and very stylish. You can usually find a large buckle on an old belt from a thrift store. Using craft cord will give it a sturdier feel, but acrylic or cotton can also be used.

Materials needed:

130 yd of worsted-weight yarn or 13 skeins of craft cord

Size F/5 (4 mm) hook or size needed to obtain gauge.

1 large belt buckle with bar across middle

Weaving needle

Gauge:

Craft cord: 14 hdc = 4"

Worsted-weight yarn: 13 hdc = 4"

Measurements:

Craft cord: 41"

Worsted-weight yarn: 44"

Directions

Ch 146.

Row 1: 1 sl st in 2nd ch from hook, 1 sl st in next 11 chs, 1 sc in next 6 chs, 1 hdc into ea ch to end. (145 sts)

Row 2: Ch 1 (count as 1st st now and throughout), turn, 1 hdc in 2nd st from hook, 1 hdc in next 126 sts, 1 sc in next 6 sts, 1 sl st in ea st to end. (145 sts) At this point, you will begin to decrease.

Row 3: Ch 1, turn, 1 sl st in 2nd st from hook, 1 sl st in next 11 sts, 1 sc in next 6 sts, 1 hdc in next 125 sts. (144 sts)

Row 4: Ch 1, turn, 1 hdc in 2nd st from hook, 1 hdc in next 126 sts, 1 sc in next 6 sts, 1 sl st into ea st to end. (143 sts)

Row 5: Ch 1, turn, 1 sl st in 2nd st from hook, 1 sl st in next 11 sts, 1 sc in next 6 sts, 1 hdc into next 123 sts. (142 sts)

Row 6: Ch 2, turn, 1 dc in 2nd st from hook, 1 dc in next 23 sts, 1 hdc in next 100 sts, 1 sc in next 6 sts, 1 sl st into ea st to end. (142 sts)

Row 7: Ch 1, turn, 1 sl st in 2nd st from hook, 1 sl st in next 11 sts, 1 sc in next 6 sts, 1 hdc in next 48 sts, 1 dc in next 72 sts. (139 sts)

Row 8:   Ch 2, turn, 1 dc in 2nd st from hook, 1 dc in next 67 sts, 1 hdc in next 57 sts, 1 sc in next 6 sts, 1 sl st in ea st to end. (139 sts)

Row 9:   Ch 1, turn, 1 sl st in 2nd st from hook, 1 sl st in next 11 sts, 1 sc in next 6 sts, 1 hdc in next 56 sts, 1 dc in next 63 sts. (138 sts)

Ch 1, work a sc edging down the sloped side of the belt. Fasten off.

Work a single crochet edging down the sloped side.

Belt buckle

Work 47 sc around the buckle, or however many sts are needed to cover it, join.

Fold the smaller end of the belt over the buckle.

Turn the belt over and secure the small end of the belt to the longer part using a weaving needle. Fasten off and weave in all ends.

Secure the small end of the belt to the longer part with a weaving needle.

It's a Wrap

Wrap sweaters are great because they can be worn as a jacket or a shirt.
This style can be worn over a T-shirt, tank, or nothing at all—be sexy with your belly out!

Materials needed:

450(515,550,600) yd or three(four,four,five) 3.5-oz
(100-g) skeins of worsted-weight yarn in color A

220(250,300,350) yd or two(two,two,three) 3.5-oz
(100-g) skeins of worsted-weight yarn in color B.

Size J/10 (6 mm) hook or size needed to obtain gauge

Weaving needle

Stitch marker

Gauge:

11 dc = 4"

Sizes:

Small (Medium, Large, X-large)

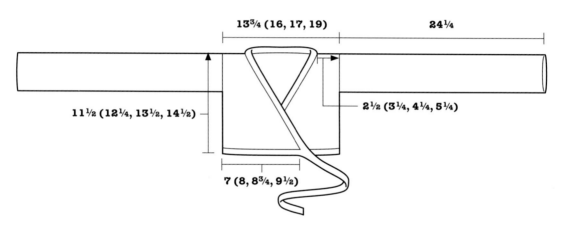

Directions

Back

Using color A, ch 41(46,51,56).

Row 1:   1 dc in 2nd ch from hook, 1 dc in ea ch to
end. [40(45,50,55) sts]

Rows 2–21(2–22,2–25,2–27):
Ch 2 (count as 1st st now and throughout),
1 dc in 2nd st from hook, 1 dc in ea ch to
end. [40(45,50,55) sts] Fasten off.

Front panels

Using color A, ch 21(23,26,28).

Row 1:   Ch 2 (count as 1st st now and throughout),
1 dc in 2nd ch from hook, 1 dc in ea ch to
end. [20(22,25,27) sts]

Rows 2–7(2–8,2–10,2–12):
Ch 2, turn, 1 dc in 2nd st from hook, 1 dc in
ea st to end. [20(22,25,27) sts]

Row 8(9,11,13):

> Ch 2, turn, 1 dc in 2nd st from hook,
> 1 dc ea st to the end, except the last st.
> [19(21,24,26) sts]

Row 9(10,12,14):

> Rep row 8. [18(20,23,25) sts]
>
> Continue to rep row 8 through row
> 20(21,23,25). [7(9,12,14) sts] Fasten off.

Rep for 2 panels.

Joining the panels

Match the top corners of the front panels with RSs facing and join with a sc seam.

Fasten off. With WSs facing, join one side of the front panel to one side of the back panel with a sc seam from row 1 to row 10(11,13,15). Fasten off.

Rep for the other side.

Match the sides of the front and back panels together and join with a single crochet seam.

Neck edging

With the garment RS out, join color B at the bottom edge of the left front panel. Work a sc edging around the neck and bottom of the joined panels, working 3 sc in ea corner, then join.

Match the corners of the front panels and join with a single crochet seam.

Join color B at the bottom edge and work a single crochet edging around.

It's a Wrap... continued

Do not fasten off. You will continue work around the top.

Rnds 1–2: Ch 1, 1 sc in 2nd st from hook, 1 sc in ea st around, join. [191(215,230,245) sts]

Row 3 (work around neck only):
Ch 1, 1 sc in 2nd st from hook, 1 sc in ea st around neck only. [107(117,126,134) sts] Do not fasten off. Now you'll begin the straps.

Finished neck and panel edging.

Straps

Ch 66(66,71,71). Work 1 hdc in 2nd ch from hook, 1 hdc in ea ch, then continue working 1 hdc in stitches across the bottom of the edging.

Work 1 half double crochet in each chain and across the bottom.

When you get to the other end, ch 66(66,71,71). Work 1 hdc in 2nd ch from hook, 1 hdc in ea ch, join to the edging. Fasten off.

Join color B in the corner of one of the straps and work 1 hdc in ea st along the bottom of both straps and across the bottom of sweater. Turn and rep to make 3 rows. Fasten off.

Sleeves

Join color A at the arm seam, work an hdc edging around, join.

Rnd 1: Ch 2 (count as 1st st now and throughout), 1 dc in ea st around, join. [41(45,48,51) sts]

Rnd 2: Ch 2, *(1 dc in next 3 sts, dec over next 2 sts), rep from * around, join. [32(36,40,42) sts]

Rnds 3–20: Rep rnd 1. Do not join, instead, work in continuous rnds through rnd 20, then join. (Use a stitch marker to keep track of your rounds.) Join color B.

Rnds 21–32: Rep rnd 1. Do not join, instead, work in continuous rnds through rnd 32, then join. Fasten off. Rep for other arm. Weave in all the ends.

Shoulder Lean

This sexy top is simple and fun! It can be made with a glittery yarn for going to a club or an acrylic yarn for a night at the movies.

Materials needed:
520(555,600) yd or three(four,four) 1.75-oz (50-g) skeins of sport-weight yarn

Size J/10 (6 mm) hook or size needed to obtain gauge

Stitch marker

Weaving needle

Gauge:
11 dc = 4"

Sizes:
Small (Medium, Large)

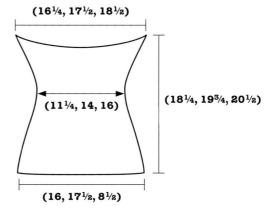

(16¼, 17½, 18½)

(11¼, 14, 16)

(18¼, 19¾, 20½)

(16, 17½, 8½)

Directions

Body
Ch 86(101,111), with right sides facing join to form a ring.

Rnd 1:   Ch 2, 1 dc in 2nd ch from hook and in ea ch around, join. [85(100,110) sts]

Rnds 2–15(2–17,2–19):
    Ch 2 (count as 1st st now and throughout, 1 dc in 1st st from hook and in ea st around. Do not join; use a st marker to mark the beginning of the first rnd, then work in continuous rnds through last rnd, join after last rnd. [85(100,110) sts]

Rnd 16(18,20):
    Using a stitch marker as a guide for the beginning of the rnd, ch 2, *(1 dc in next 5 sts, dec over the next 2 sts), rep from * around, join. [74(87,95) sts]

Rnds 17–18(19–20,21–22):
    Rep rnd 2. [74(87,95) sts]

Rnd 19(21,23):
    Rep rnd 16. [64(75,82) sts]

Rnds 20–21 (22–23, 24–25):
Rep rnd 2. [64(75,82) sts]

Rnd 22(24,26):
Rep rnd 16. [56(65,71) sts]

Rnds 23–25(25–27, 27–29):
Rep rnd 2. [56(65,71) sts] Do not fasten off.
Now begin the front of the top.

Front small

Row 1:   Ch 2 (count as 1st st now and throughout),
turn, 1 dc in 1st st from hook, 1 dc in next
25 sts. [27 sts]

Row 2:   Ch 2, turn, 1 dc in 2nd st from hook, 1 dc
in next 4 sts, *(2 dc in next st, 1 dc in next
5 sts), rep from * twice, 1 dc in ea st to end.
[31 sts]

Row 3:   Ch 2, turn, 1 dc in 2nd st from hook, 1 dc
in next 4 sts, *(2 dc in next st, 1 dc in next
5 sts), repeat from * 3 times, 2 dc in last st.
[36 sts]

Row 4:   Ch 2, turn, 1 dc in 2nd st from hook, 1 dc
in next 4 sts, *(2 dc in next st, 1 dc in next
5 sts), rep from * 4 times [41 sts]

Rows   Ch 2, turn, 1 dc in 2nd st from hook,
5–10:   1 dc in ea st to end. [44 sts]
Fasten off.

Back small

With the back of the top facing you, join the yarn
in the 2nd st from the 1st row of the front.

Row 1:   Ch 2, 1 dc in 1st st from hook, 1 dc in next
25 sts. [26 sts]

Row 2:   Ch 2, turn, 1 dc in 1st st from hook, 1 dc
in next 4 sts *(2 dc in next st, 1 dc in next
5 sts), rep from * twice, 2 dc in next st, 1 dc
in last 2 sts. [31sts]

Row 3:   Ch 2, turn, 1 dc in 2nd st from hook, 1 dc
in next 4 sts, *(2 dc in next st, 1 dc in next

5 sts), rep from * 3 times, 2 dc in last st.
[36 sts]

Row 4:   Rep row 2. [41(45,52) sts]

Front medium

Row 1:   Ch 2 (count as 1st st now and throughout),
turn, 1 dc in 1st st from hook, 1 dc in next
32) sts. [34 sts]

Row 2:   Ch 2, turn, 1 dc in 2nd st from hook, 1 dc
in next 4 sts, *(2 dc in next st, 1 dc in next
5 sts), rep from* 3 times, 2 dc in next st,
1 dc in last st. [37 sts]

Row 3:   Ch 2, turn, 1 dc in 2nd st from hook, 1 dc
in next 4 sts, *(2 dc in next st, 1 dc in next
5 sts), rep from* 4 times, 2 dc in last st.
[43 sts]

Row 4:   Ch 2, turn, 1 dc in 2nd st from hook, 1 dc
in next 4 sts, *(2 dc in next st, 1 dc in next
5 sts), rep from* 4 times. [50 sts]

Rows   Ch 2, turn, 1 dc in 2nd st from hook, 1 dc in
5–12:   ea st to end. [50 sts]

Back medium

With the back of the top facing you, join the yarn in the
2nd st from the 1st row of the front.

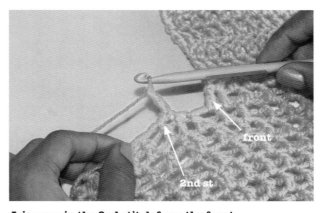

Join yarn in the 2nd stitch from the front.

Row 1:	Ch 2, 1 dc in 1st st from hook, 1 dc in next [30 sts]
Row 2:	Ch 2, turn, 1 dc in 1st st from hook, 1 dc in next 4 sts *(2 dc in next st, 1 dc in next 5 sts), rep from* 3 times, 2 dc in last st. [36 sts]
Row 3:	Ch 2, turn, 1 dc in 2nd st from hook, 1 dc in next 4 sts *(2 dc in next st, 1 dc in next 5 sts), rep from* 4 times. [41 sts]
Row 4:	Rep row 2. [48 sts]
Rows 5–14:	Ch 2, turn, 1 dc in 2nd st from hook, 1 dc in ea st to end. [48 sts]. Fasten off.

Front large

Row 1:	Ch 2 (count as 1st st now and throughout), turn, 1 dc in 1st st from hook, 1 dc in next 34) sts. [36 sts]
Row 2:	Ch 2, turn, 1 dc in 2nd st from hook, 1 dc in next 4 sts, *(2 dc in next st, 1 dc in next 5 sts), rep from* 4 times. [41 sts]
Row 3:	Ch 2, turn, 1 dc in 2nd st from hook, 1 dc in next 4 sts, *(2 dc in next st, 1 dc in next 5 sts), rep from* 4 times, 2 dc in next st, 1 dc in last 4 sts. [47 sts]
Row 4:	Ch 2, turn, 1 dc in 2nd st from hook, 1 dc in next 4 sts, *(2 dc in next st, 1 dc in next 5 sts), rep from* 5 times, 2 dc in next st, 1 dc in last 4 sts. [54 sts]
Rows 5–14:	Ch 2, turn, 1 dc in 2nd st from hook, 1 dc in ea st to end. [54 sts]

Back large

With the back of the top facing you, join the yarn in the 2nd st from the 1st row of the front.

Row 1:	Ch 2, 1 dc in 1st st from hook, 1 dc in next 30 sts. [32 sts]

Row 2:	Ch 2, turn, 1 dc in 1st st from hook, 1 dc in next 4 sts *(2 dc in next st, 1 dc in next 5 sts), rep from * 3 times, 2 dc in, next st, 1 dc in last 2 sts. [38 sts]
Row 3:	Ch 2, turn, 1 dc in 2nd st from hook, 1 dc in next 4 sts *(2 dc in next st, 1 dc in next 5 sts), rep from * 4 times, 2 dc in next st, 1 dc in last 2 sts. [43 sts]
Row 4:	Rep row 2. [52 sts]
Rows 5–16:	Ch 2, turn, 1 dc in 2nd st from hook, 1 dc in ea st to end. [52 sts]. Fasten off.

Joining the front and back

Join the corners of the front and back with a weaving needle by sewing together the corners only. Fasten off.

Sleeves

Join the corners of the yarn at the armhole seam, work a sc edging around, and join. Fasten off.

Rep for other sleeve. Weave in all ends.

Join the corners of the front and back with a weaving needle.

That Girl

This long sweater is stylish and sexy. It goes great with jeans or a short skirt.
The elastic around the middle helps keep a snug fit.

Materials needed:

300(400,500,600) yd or two
(two,three,three) 4.5-oz (127-g) skeins
of worsted-weight yarn in color A

150(165,180,190) yd or one 4.5-oz
(127-g) skein *each* of worsted-weight
yarn in colors B, C, and D

Size H/8 (5 mm) hook or size
needed to obtain gauge.

Stitch marker

Weaving needle

Round cord elastic

Gauge:

8 sc (ch 1 sps) = 4"

Sizes:

Small (Medium, Large, X-large)

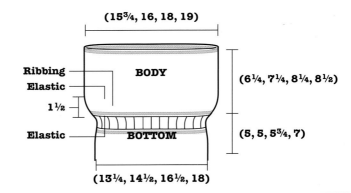

Directions

Ribbing

Using color A, ch 6.

Row 1:   1 sc in 2nd ch from hook, 1 sc in ea ch
             to end. (5 sts)

Rows 2–82(2–92,2–106,2–117):
             Ch 1 (count as 1 st now and throughout
             ribbing), turn (work in back loops only now
             and throughout ribbing) 1 sc in 2nd st from
             hook, 1 sc in ea st to end. (5 sts)

With the RSs facing, join the 2 smaller sides with a sl st
seam to form a ring.

Ch 1, then work a sc edging all the way around one side
of the ribbing (85, 93, 106, 119 sts).

Weave elastic through the edging. Do not pull the
elastic tight. Cover (see page 38). Fasten off.

Do not fasten off. Now you'll begin the tube.

Work a single crochet edging around the ribbing.

That Girl... continued

Tube

Rnd 1: Ch 1, 1 sc in 1st st from hook, 1 sc in next 2 sts, *(2 sc in next st, 1 sc in next 3 sts), rep from * around, join. [107(115,132,148) sts]

For Small and Medium, join color B. For Large and X-large, continue working with color A.

Rnd 2: Ch 2, 1 sc in 2nd from hook, *(ch 1, sk next st, 1 sc in next st), rep from * around, join. [53(57,66,74) sts]

Rnds 3–5: Ch 2, *(sk next sc, 1 sc in next ch sp, ch 1), rep from * around. Do not join, instead, work in continuous rnds through rnd 5, join with a sl st at the end of last rnd. (Use a stitch marker to keep track of the rnds.) [53(57, 66,74) sts]

For Small and Medium, join color A. For Large and X-large, join color B.

Rnds 6–9: Rep rnd 3. [53 (57, 66,74) sts]

For Small and Medium, join color C. For Large and X-large, join color A.

Rnds 10–13: Rep rnd 3. [53(57, 66,74) sts]

For Small and Medium, join color A. For Large and X-large, join color C.

14–17: Rep rnd 3. 53(57, 66,74) sts]

For Small and Medium, join color D. For Large and X-large, join color A.

Rnds 18–21: Rep rnd 3. 53(57, 66,74) sts]

For Small and Medium, join color A. For Large and X-large, join color D.

Rnds 22–25: Rep rnd 3. 53(57, 66,74) sts]

Fasten off for Small and Medium.

Continue for Large and X-large. Join color A.

Rnds 26–29: Rep rnd 3. [66(74) sts] Join color A.

Rnds 30–33: Rep rnd 3. [66(74) sts]

Final rnd for all sizes: Ch 1 (count as 1st st), 1 sc in ea sc and ch sp around, join. [108(114,132,148) sts]

Weave elastic through last rnd (do not pull the elastic) and cover using color A (see page 38). Work a sc edging around the other side of the ribbing. Weave elastic through the edging and cover. Do not fasten off. Now you'll begin the bottom.

Bottom

Rnds 1–3(1–3,1–5,1–7): Ch 2, 1 dc in 1st st from hook and in ea st around. Do not join, instead, continue working dc in continuous rnds and join at the end of last rnd. (Use a stitch marker at the end of rnd 3 to keep track of the rnds.) [81(92,107,117) sts] Join color B.

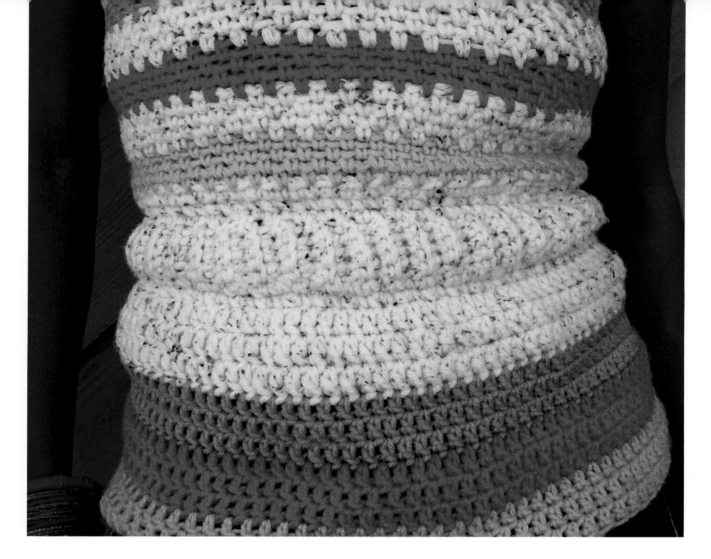

Rnds 4–6(4–6,6–8,8–10):
Ch 2, 1 dc in ea st around. Do not join, instead, work in continuous rnds and join at the end of last rnd. [82(92,107,117) sts] Join color C.

Rnds 7–9(7–9,9–11,11–13):
Ch 2, 1 dc in ea st around. Do not join, instead, work in continuous rnds and join at the end of last rnd. [82(92,107,117) sts] Join color D.

Rnds 10–12(10–12,12–14,14–16):
Ch 2, 1 dc in ea st around. Do not join, instead, work in continuous rnds and join at the end of last rnd. [82(92,107,117) sts] Fasten off. Weave in all ends. Feel free to make it larger by adding more rows in color A.

Baby Doll

This baby doll top can be made with cotton yarn and worn in the summer with a pair of shorts or made with acrylic or wool and worn with your favorite pair of jeans in winter. Elastic is added in the middle for a snug fit.

Materials needed:

325(360,450,500,560) yd or two(two,three,four,four) 2.5-oz (70.9-g) skeins of worsted-weight yarn in color A

80(100,120,150,180) yd or one to two 2.5-oz (70.9-g) skeins of worsted-weight yarn in color B

Size F/11 (8 mm) hook or size needed to obtain gauge

Weaving needle

Round cord elastic

Gauge:

14 dc = 4"

Sizes:

X-small (Small, Medium, Large, X-large)

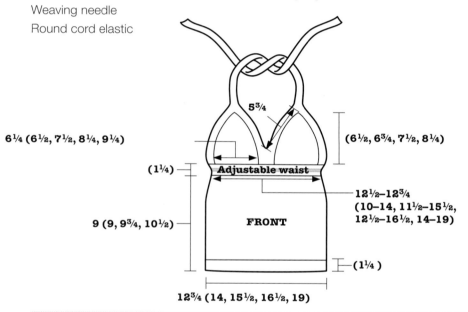

Directions

Making the cups

Using color A, ch 11, turn.

Row 1:   1 dc in 2nd ch from hook, 1 dc in ea ch to end. (10 sts)

Row 2:   Ch 2, (count as 1st st now and throughout), turn, 1 dc in 2nd st from hook, 1 dc in next 7 sts, 2 dc in next st [1 dc, 1 tr, 1 dc] in next st,

Baby Doll... continued

Do not turn, begin picking up stitches, and continue working across the opposite side of the foundation chain.

(do not turn, continue working across opposite side of foundation ch) 2 dc in next st, 1 dc in next 9 chs to end. (25 sts)

Row 3: Ch 2, turn, 1 dc in 2nd st from hook, 1 dc in next 9 sts, 2 dc in next st, [1 dc, 1 tr, 1 dc] in next st, 2 dc in next st, 1 dc in ea st to end. (29 sts)

Row 4: Ch 2, turn, 1 dc in 2nd st from hook, 1 dc in next 10 sts, 2 dc in next 2 sts, [1 dc, 1 tr, 1 dc] in next st, 2 dc in next 2 sts, 1 dc in ea st to end. (35 sts)

Row 5: Ch 2, turn, 1 dc in 2nd st from hook, 1 dc in next 13 sts, 2 dc in next 2 sts, [1 dc, 1 tr, 1 dc] in next st, 2 dc in next 2 sts, 1 dc in ea st to end. (41 sts)

Row 6: Ch 2, turn, 1 dc in 2nd st from hook, 1 dc in next 17 sts, 2 dc in next st, [1 dc, 1 tr, 1 dc] in next st, 2 dc in next st, 1 dc in ea st to end. (45 sts)

Continue for Small, Medium, Large, X-large.

Row 7: Ch 2, turn, 1 dc in 2nd st from hook, 1 dc in next 19 sts, 2 dc in next st, [1 dc, 1 tr, 1 dc] in next st, 2 dc in next st, 1 dc in ea st to end. (49 sts)

Continue for Medium, Large, X-large.

Row 8: Ch 2, turn, 1 dc in 2nd st from hook, 1 dc in next 21 sts, 2 dc in next st, [1 dc, 1 tr, 1 dc]

in next st, 2 dc in next st, 1 dc in ea st to end. (53 sts)

Continue for Large, X-large.

Row 9: Ch 2, turn, 1 dc in 2nd st from hook, 1 dc in next 22 sts, 2 dc in next st, [1 dc, 1 tr, 1 dc] in next st, 2 dc in next st, 1 dc in ea st to end. (56 sts)

Continue for X-large.

Row 10: Ch 2 , turn, 1 dc in 2nd st from hook, 1 dc in next 25 sts, 2 dc in next st, [1 dc, 1 tr, 1 dc] in next st, 2 dc in next st, 1 dc in ea st to end. (61 sts) For all sizes, fasten off.

Making the trim and straps

With the point of the cup facing left, join color B at the right corner, ch 1, and begin working a sc edging around the cup. When you get to the tr of the previous row, begin the strap. Ch 80, then work 1 dc in each ch, with 1 hdc in the last ch. Join the strap with a sl st to the tr of the previous row of the cup. Continue working sc edging around cup, with 3 sc in ea corner, join. Fasten off.

Make one more cup and rep trim and strap (for a total of 2 cups).

When you get to the triple crochet of the previous row, chain 80 for the strap.

To make the top strap, work 1 double crochet in each chain, then join the strap to triple crochet of the previous row with a slip stitch.

Joining the cups

With RSs facing, match the ends (with the point facing left) and join color A at the bottom right edge. Work a sl

With the points facing left and right sides facing, match the cups; join color B at the bottom edge, and join with a slip-stitch seam.

st seam in 1st 6(6,6,7,8) sts. Fasten off.

Body

With the RS facing you and the points facing down, join color B at the corner of the left cup. Ch 51(51,56,61,71). Join chain with a sl st in the corner of the other cup. Please make sure the back strap is not twisted when joining it to the front.

Rnd 1: Ch 1, 1 hdc in ea st of edging on both cups, 1 hdc in ea ch st around back join. [93 (100,114,126,133) sts] Weave elastic through rnd 1, cover (see page 38), and join (keep the bunched-up section toward the back).

Rnd 2: Ch 1, 1 hdc in 2nd st from hook, 1 hdc in ea st around, join. [93(101,115,127,133) sts] Weave elastic through rnd 2 and cover. Join color A.

Rnd 3: Ch 3, *(1 tr in next 2 sts, 2 tr in next st), rep from * around, join. [127(134,154, 169,182) sts]

Rnds 4–10(4–10,4–11,4–11,4–12): Ch 3, 1 tr in 2nd st from hook, 1 tr in ea st around, join. [128(134,154,169,183) sts] Join color B.

Rnds 11–16(11–16,12–17,13–18,13-20): Ch 1, 11 sc in 2nd st from hook, sc in ea st around, join. [128(134,154,169,183) sts] At this point you can add more rows if you'd like it longer. Fasten off. Weave in all ends.

Bangles — 1

YOUNG BUCK

These simple accessories are a staple in any wardrobe. Wear 1 or 20—the more the better!

Materials needed:

50 yd or one 67-oz (19-g) skein of metallic, sport-weight or nylon yarn

Size F/5 (4 mm) hook

Weaving needle

Plastic bangles

Directions

Work 70 sc around the bangle (or however many sts are needed to cover it), join. (70 sts) Fasten off. Weave in ends.

Cover the bangle with single crochet stitches.

Lil' Ma

The thing I love about this top is that it can be made in cotton yarn for a sporty look or a textured yarn for a night on the town. I've been asked, "Where are the bottoms?" but this sexy top can be worn with pants, under a shirt as an accent, or even under one of the mesh-style tunics in this book.

Materials needed:

170(200,210,225,240) yd or two 2.5-oz (70.9-g) skeins of worsted-weight yarn in color A

100(110,115,120,120) yd or one 2.5-oz (70.9-g) skein of worsted-weight yarn in color B

Size F/11 (8 mm) hook or size needed to obtain gauge

Weaving needle

Gauge:

14 dc = 4"

Sizes:

X-small (Small, Medium, Large, X-large)

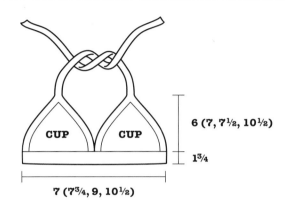

Directions

Making the cups

Using color A, ch 11.

Row 1:   1 dc in 2nd ch from hook, 1 dc in ea ch to end. (10 sts)

Row 2:   Ch 2 (count as 1st st now and throughout), turn, 1 dc in 2nd st from hook, 1 dc in next 7 sts, 2 dc in next st, [1 dc, 1 tr, 1 dc] in next st (do not turn, continue working across opposite side of foundation ch), 2 dc in next st, 1 dc in next 9 chs to end. (24 sts)

Continue working across the opposite side of the foundation chain.

Row 3:   Ch 2, turn, 1 dc in 2nd st from hook, 1 dc in next 9 sts, 2 dc in next st, [1 dc, 1 tr, 1 dc] in next st, 2 dc in next st, 1 dc in ea st to end. (29 sts)

Row 4:   Ch 2, turn, 1 dc in 2nd st from hook, 1 dc in next 10 sts, 2 dc in next 2 sts, [1 dc, 1 tr, 1 dc] in next st, 2 dc in next 2 sts, 1 dc in ea st to end. (35 sts)

Row 5:   Ch 2, turn, 1 dc in 2nd st from hook, 1 dc in next 13 sts, 2 dc in next 2 sts, [1 dc, 1 tr, 1 dc] in next st, 2 dc in next 2 sts, 1 dc in ea st to end. (41 sts)

Row 6:   Ch 2, turn, 1 dc in 2nd st from hook, 1 dc in next 17 sts, 2 dc in next st, [1 dc, 1 tr, 1 dc] in next st, 2 dc in next st, 1 dc in ea st to end. (45 sts)

Continue for Small, Medium, Large, X-large.

Row 7:   Ch 2, turn, 1 dc in 2nd st from hook, 1 dc in next 19 sts, 2 dc in next st, [1 dc, 1 tr, 1 dc] in next st, 2 dc in next st, 1 dc in ea st to end. (49 sts)

Continue for Medium, Large, X-Large.

Row 8:   Ch 2, turn, 1 dc in 2nd st from hook, 1 dc in next 21 sts, 2 dc in next st, [1 dc, 1 tr, 1 dc] in next st, 2 dc in next st, 1 dc in ea st to end. (53 sts)

Continue for Large, X-Large.

Row 9:   Ch 2 , turn, 1 dc in 2nd st from hook, 1 dc in next 22 sts, 2 dc in next st, [1 dc, 1 tr, 1 dc] in next st, 2 dc in next st, 1 dc in ea st to end. (56 sts)

Continue for X-large.

Row 10:   Ch 2, turn, 1 dc in 2nd st from hook, 1 dc in next 25 sts, 2 dc in next st, [1 dc, 1 tr, 1 dc] in next st, 2 dc in next st, 1 dc in ea st to end. (61 sts) Do not fasten off. Now you will begin the trim and straps.

Making the trim and top strap

Join color B.

Ch 1, and work a hdc edging until you come to the tr in previous row. Ch 80, then work 1 dc in next 80 chs. Join the strap in the tr of the previous row with a sl st. Continue working hdc edging all the way around the cup, working 3 hdc in each corner, join. Fasten off.

Work a half double crochet edging to the triple crochet of the previous row, then chain 80.

Work 1 double crochet in each chain, but 1 half double crochet in the last chain; then join the strap in the triple crochet of the previous row.

Make one more cup and rep trim and strap (for a total of 2 cups).

Joining the cups

With the RSs facing, match the ends (with the points facing left) and join color B at the bottom right edge. Work a sl st seam in the 1st 6 sts. Fasten off.

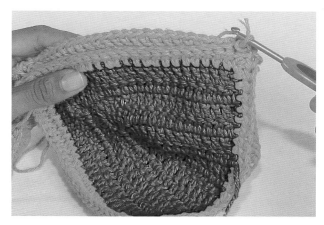

With the points facing left and right sides facing, match up the cups, join color B at the bottom edge, and join with a slip-stitch seam.

Side straps

With the RS facing you and the points of the cups facing down, join color B at the corner of the right cup.

Ch 80, then work 1 hdc in ea ch. At the end of the ch, continue to work 1 hdc in ea st across the bottom of the cups.

Work 1 half double crochet in each chain, then continue to work 1 half double crochet in each stitch across the bottom of the cups.

When you reach the end of the other side, ch 80, turn, work 1 hdc in ea ch, then join.

Fasten off, then join the yarn at any corner of either of the side straps. Work 2 more rows of hdc along each of the straps and previous rows. Fasten off. Weave in all the ends.

Fat Gold Chain

This has to be my favorite pattern in the entire book! It took me quite a while to get it to look exactly like a real chain; but one day I was watching Martha Stewart, and she was talking about a craft called lanyards and that was exactly what I needed! Thanks, Martha!

Materials needed:
80 yd of gold metallic cord (trim)
Size F/5 (4 mm) hook or size needed to obtain gauge
Weaving needle

Gauge:
14 dc = 4"

Directions

Making the strips
Ch 201

Row 1:   1 dc in ea ch to end. (200 sts) Fasten off.
Rep for a total of 2 strips.

Folding the strips together
Place one strip across the other. Join them by weaving the ends together.

Fold the strips over each other, alternating each strip.

Fold the strips over each other, alternating each strip.

Join the strip ends with a weaving needle. Join both ends of the chain with a weaving needle. Weave in the ends.

Place one strip across the other and weave the ends together.

N'Digi Bag

This pouch pattern was inspired by one of my belts, but I actually got the pattern and sizing from an indigenous people's craft book. You can add fringes for a little flair.

Materials needed:

150 yd of craft cord or worsted-weight yarn in color A

75 yd of craft cord or worsted-weight yarn in color B

Size H/10 (6 mm) hook or size needed to obtain gauge

Weaving needle

Sewing needle

1 snap

sewing thread to match yarn

Gauge:

Craft cord, 14 sc = 4"

Worsted-weight yarn, 16 sc = 4"

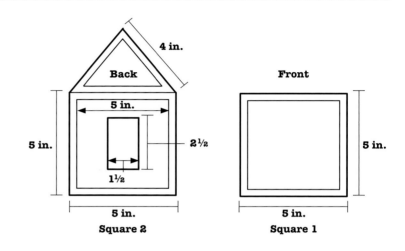

Directions

Squares

Using color A, ch 16.

Row 1:   1 sc in 2nd ch from hook, 1 sc in ea ch to end. (15 sts)

Rows 2–16:   Ch 1 (count as 1st st now and throughout), turn, 1 sc in 2nd st from hook, 1 sc in ea st to end. (16 sc) Fasten off.

Join color B at any corner. Ch 1, then work a sc edging around the panel, working 3 sc in ea corner. Fasten off. Rep once more for a total of 2 squares.

Triangle

Using color A, ch 14.

Row 1:   1 sc in 2nd ch from hook, 1 sc in ea ch to end. (13 sts) You will now begin to decrease.

Row 2:   Ch 1 (count as 1st st now and throughout), turn, 1 sc in 2nd st from hook, 1 sc in next 10 sts. (12 sc)

Row 3:   Ch 1, turn, 1 sc in 2nd st from hook, 1 sc in next 9 sts. (11 sc)

Row 4:   Ch 1, turn, 1 sc in 2nd st from hook, 1 sc in next 7 sts. (9 sc)

Row 5:   Ch 1, turn, 1 sc in 2nd st from hook, 1 sc in next 5 sts. (7 sc)

Row 6:   Ch 1, turn, 1 sc in 2nd st from hook, 1 sc in next 3 sts. (5 sc)

Row 7:   Ch 1, turn, 1 sc in 2nd st from hook, 1 sc in next 2 sts. (4 sc)

Row 8:   Ch 1, turn, 1 sc in 2nd st from hook, 1 sc in next st. (2 sc)

Triangle Edging

Ch 1, work a sc edging around the triangle, working 3 sc into ea corner and in the tip, join. Join color B. (38 sts)

Rnd 1: Ch 1, work 1 sc in ea st around, working 3 sc in ea corner st and in the tip, join. Fasten off. (43 sts)

Pouch Strap

Using color A, ch 9.

Row 1: 1 sc in 2nd ch from hook and ea ch to end. (8 sts)

Row 2: Ch 1 (count as first st now and throughout strap), turn, 1 sc in 2nd st from hook and ea st to end. (8 sts)

Rows 3–5: Rep row 2. (8 sts) Fasten off.

Center the shorter sides of the strap on the top and bottom edges of one of the squares. Secure the ends down using a weaving needle.

Center the strap on the outside of one of the squares. Sew the short ends to the edges of the square.

Joining the squares and triangle

Match the corners of the triangle with the inside of the
second square. Using color B, sew the edges together
using a weaving needle to weave in and out of ea st.
Match the squares together with the WSs facing
and weave the edges together.

Using color B, join the triangle and the second square.

Adding a snap to the pouch

Place one side of the snap directly under the tip of the
WS of the triangle. Sew it down using sewing thread.

Sew on the snap using similar color thread.

Center the other side of the snap on the front side of the first square so that it matches up with the first side of the snap, then sew it on.

Join second part of the snap to the center of the first square, l matching it up with the first part of the snap.

Adding fringe

You will be adding a single-strand fringe to each st along the bottom of the pouch. Cut ea strand of yarn 20" long. Fold a strand in half, then use your hook to pull the loop through the st. Take the loose ends of the strand and pull them through the loop. Pull gently to tighten the knot. After you have added all the fringe, trim the ends even.

Add fringe along the bottom of the pouch.

Nuff Gluvs

These long fingerless gloves can be worn with a T-shirt, tank top,
or short-sleeve denim jacket. You can wear one or two at a time! Rock on!

Materials needed:

230(250,300) yd or two 3-oz (85-g) skeins of light or
regular worsted-weight yarn

Size H/8 (5 mm) hook or size needed to obtain gauge.

Weaving needle

Round cord elastic

Gauge:

14 hdc = 4"

Sizes:

Small (Medium, Large)

Directions

Ribbing

Ch 11

Row 1:   1 sc in 2nd ch from hook, 1 sc in ea ch to end. (10 sts)

Rows 2–30(2–33,2–36):   Ch 1 (count as 1st st now and throughout), turn (work in back loops only now and throughout ribbing), 1 sc in 2nd st from hook, 1 sc in ea st to end. (10 sts)

With RSs facing, join the two shorter sides with a sl st seam. Turn ribbing to RS, ch 1, work a sc edging around, join. Weave elastic through ribbing and cover. Fasten off.

Join the yarn at the other side of the ribbing seam. Work a sc edging around, join. Weave elastic through edging and cover. Do not fasten off. Begin working on arm.

Arm

Rnd 1:   Ch 1, 1 hdc in ea st around, join. [32(36,39) sts]

Rnds 2–20(2–21,2–23):   Ch 1, 1 hdc in ea st around; do not join but continue to work in continuous rnds through the last rnd, join after last rnd. [32(36,39) sts]

Rnd 21(22,24):   Ch 1, *(1 hdc in next 3 sts, dec over next 2 sts), rep from * around, join. [24(28,31) sts]

Rnds 22–30(23–31,25–33):   Ch 1, 1 hdc in ea st around; do not join but continue to work in continuous rnds through last rnd, join after last rnd. [24(28,31) sts]

Rnd 31(32,34):   Ch 1, *(1 sc in next 7 sts, dec over next 2 sts), rep from * around. Do not join. [20(25,28) sts]

Rnds 32–37(33–38,35–40):   Ch 1, 1 hdc in ea st around; do not join but continue to work in continuous rnds through last rnd. Join with a sl st at end last rnd. [20(25,28) sts]

At this point, you can add more sc rows if you need to make the gloves longer. Do not fasten off. Now you will begin the hand.

Hand

Rows 1–8(1–8,1–9):   Ch 1, turn, 1 hdc in 2nd st from hook, 1 hdc in ea st to end, do not join. [20(25,28) sts] Fasten off.

Joining the thumb and adding elastic

Match the left corners and join the corners only, on the WS, with a weaving needle. Weave elastic through the last round and cover (see page 38). Fasten off. Rep the entire pattern once more for a total of 2 gloves. Weave in all ends.

Dawta

This halter top was inspired by the backless Indian tops known as cholis.
It can be made in cotton yarn for warm weather or in acrylic or wool for the colder months.

Materials needed:

250(300,340,380) yd or two to three
3-oz (85-g) skeins of worsted-weight
yarn in color A

75(90,105,120) yd or one 3-oz (85-g)
skein in color B

Size F/11 (4 mm) hook for panels
and H/8(5 mm) hook for body or sizes
needed to obtain gauge

Gauge:

Size F hook, 13 dc = 4"

Size H hook, 12 dc = 4"

Sizes:

Small (Medium, Large, X-large)

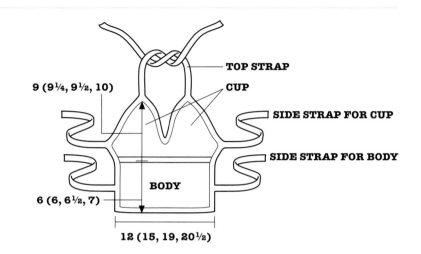

Directions

Making the cups

Using color A and size F hook, ch 21.

Row 1:   1 dc in 2nd ch from hook, 1 dc in ea ch to
end. (20 sts)

Row 2:   Ch 2 (count as 1st st now and throughout),
turn, 1 dc in 2nd st from hook, 1 dc in next 16
sts, 2 dc in next st, [1 dc, 1 tr, 1 dc] in next st,
(do not turn; continue working across opposite
side of foundation ch) 2 dc in next st, 1 dc ea
ch to end. (44 sts)

Row 3:   Ch 2, turn, 1 dc in 2nd st from hook,
1 dc in next 18 sts, 2 dc in next st, [1 dc,
1 tr, 1 dc] in next st, 2 dc in next st, 1 dc in
ea st to end. (48 sts)

Row 4:   Ch 2, turn, 1 dc in 2nd st from hook,
1 dc in next 19 sts, 2 dc in next 2 sts,
[1 dc, 1 tr, 1 dc] in next st, 2 dc in next 2 sts,
1 dc in ea st to end. (54 sts)

**Continue working across the opposite side of the
foundation chain.**

Row 5:   Ch 2, turn, 1 dc in 2nd st from hook,
1 dc in next 22 sts, 2 dc in next 2 sts,
[1 dc, 1 tr, 1 dc] in next st, 2 dc in next 2 sts,
1 dc in ea st to end. (60 sts)

Row 6:   Ch 2, turn, 1 dc in 2nd st from hook,
1 dc in next 26 sts, 2 dc in next st,
[1 dc, 1 tr, 1 dc] in next st, 2 dc in next st,
1 dc in ea st to end. (64 sts)

Continue for Medium, Large, X-large.

Row 7:   Ch 2, turn, 1 dc in 2nd st from hook,
          1 dc in next 28 sts, 2 dc in next st, [1 dc,
          1 tr, 1 dc] in next st, 2 dc in next st, 1 dc in
          ea st to end. (68 sts)

Continue for Large, X-large.

Row 8:   Ch 2, turn, 1 dc in 2nd st from hook,
          1 dc in next 29 sts, 2 dc in next 2 sts,
          [1 dc, 1 tr, 1 dc] in next st, 2 dc in next 2 sts,
          1 dc in ea st to end. (74 sts)

Continue for X-large.

Row 9:   Ch 2, turn, 1 dc in 2nd st from hook,
          1 dc in next 33 sts, 2 dc in next st, [1 dc,
          1 tr, 1 dc] in next st, 2 dc in next st, 1 dc in
          ea st to end. (78 sts) Fasten off.

Making side straps for the cups

Join color A in the 8th st of the last row of the cup.

**To begin the side strap, join color A in 8th stitch of the
last row in the cup.**

Row 1: Ch 2 (count as 1st st now and throughout), 1 dc in next 11(11,12,13) sts. [12(12,13,14) sts]

Row 2: Ch 2, turn, 1 dc in 2nd st from hook, 1 dc in next 9(9,11,12) sts. [11(11,12,13) sts]

Row 3: Ch 2, turn, 1 dc in 2nd st from hook, 1 dc in next 8(9,10,11) sts. [9(10,11,12) sts]

Row 4: Ch 2, turn, 1 dc in 2nd st from hook, 1 dc in next 5(6,7,8) sts. [7(8,9,10) sts]

Row 5: Ch 2, turn, 1 dc in 2nd st from hook, 1 dc in next 3(4,5,6) sts. [5(6,7,8) sts]

Row 6: Ch 2, turn, 1 dc in 2nd st from hook, 1 dc in next 1(2,3,4) sts. [3(4,5,6) sts]

Continue for Medium (Large, X-large).

Row 7: Ch 2, turn, 1 dc in 2nd st from hook, 1 dc in next 1(2,3) sts. [3(4,5) sts]

Continue for Large (X-large).

Row 8: Ch 2, turn, 1 dc in 2nd st from hook, 1 dc in next 1(2) sts. [3(4) sts]

Continue for X-large

Row 9: Ch 2, turn, 1 dc in 2nd st from hook, 1 dc in next st. (2 sts)

Rep panel and strap for a total of 2 cups.

Joining the cups

Match ends (with points facing left), join color A at the bottom right edge.

Work a sl st seam in 1st 10(12,14,16) sts. Fasten off.

Try top on and position it under your breasts to see how low the top is cut. If you'd like to close it some more, add as many sl sts as you'd like.

With RS facing you and the points facing down, join color A at the right edge of the right cup. Work an hdc edging along bottom of cups.

Do not fasten off. Now you will begin to work on the body.

Match ends with the points facing left.

Body

Switch to the H hook.

Row 1: Ch 2 (count as 1st st now and throughout), turn, 1 hdc in 2nd ch from hook, 1 hdc in ea hdc to end. [40(48,55,60) sts]

Rows 2–12(2–12,2–13,2–14): Ch 2, turn, 1 dc in 2nd ch from hook, 1 dc in ea hdc to end. [40(48,55,60) sts]

Fasten off. Join color B. Now you will begin to work an hdc edging around the entire top as well as add the side and top straps.

Side straps for body

As you work the edging, when you get to row 3 (4,5) of the body (about 15,16,17 sts), ch 61(71,71,81).

When you get to row 3(4,5), ch 61(71,71,81)

Row 1:   1 dc in 2nd ch from hook, 1 dc in ea ch to end. [60(70,70,80) sts] Join the strap to the body and continue the hdc edging around the body. When you get to the end of the side strap for the first cup, ch 71.

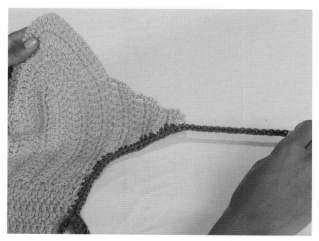

When you get to the end of the side strap for the first cup, chain 71.

Row 2:   1 dc in 2nd ch from hook, 1 dc in ea ch to end. (70 sts) Join new strap to the edge of the side strap and continue working the hdc edging around the body until you get to the tr in the tip of the cup.

Top straps

Starting at the tr, ch 81.

Row 1:   1 dc in 2nd ch from hook, 1 dc in ea ch to end. (80 sts).

Join the strap in the tr of the cup and continue working the hdc edging around the top. Join, then fasten off.

Rep strap for other cup and other side. Fasten off and weave in the ends.

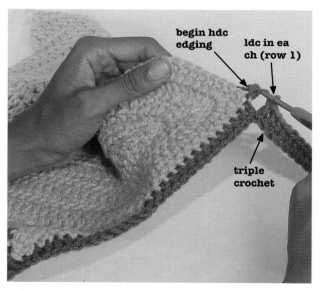

Join the top strap in the triple crochet in the cup.

Proteck Ya Neck

A nice scarf can accentuate any coat, but it can also be worn with a T-shirt or long-sleeved shirt as part of an outfit.

Materials needed:
130 yd or one 3-oz (85-g) skein *each* of worsted-weight yarn in color A and color B

Size K/10 1/2 (6.5 mm) hook or size needed to obtain gauge

Weaving needle

Gauge:
9 sc = 4"

Directions
Using color A, ch 17.

Row 1: 1 sc in 2nd ch from hook, 1 sc in ea ch to end. (16 sts)

Row 2: Ch 2 (count as 1st st now and throughout), turn, 1 sc in 1st st from hook,*(ch 1, sk next sc, 1 sc in next st), rep from * 6 times, ch 1, 1 sc in the row-end st. (10 sc)

Rows 3–4: Ch 2, *(1 sc in next ch sp, ch 1, sk next sc), rep from * to end, working 1 sc in row-end st. (10 sc) Join color B.

Rows 5–8: Rep row 3. Join color A.

Rows 9–12: Rep row 3. Join color B.

Rows 13–16: Rep row 3. Join color A.

Rows 17–20: Rep row 3. Join color B.

Rows 21–51: Rep row 3. Join color A.

Rows 52–139: Rep row 3. Join color B.

Rows 140–170: Rep row 3. Join color A.

Rows 171–174: Rep row 3. Join color B.

Rows 175–178: Rep row 3. Join color A.

Rows 179–182: Rep row 3. Join color B.

Rows 183–186: Rep row 3. Join color A.

Rows 187–190: Rep row 3. Fasten off. Weave in all the ends.

Throw Back

The first time I saw this style tank was in Jamaica. It's cool enough to wear in the summer. It can be made in sports colors to resemble a jersey.

Materials needed:

500(550,600,650,700) yd or two (all sizes) 7-oz (198-g) skeins of worsted-weight yarn in color A

75 yd or one 7-oz (198-g) skein of worsted-weight yarn in color B

Size J/10 (6 mm) crochet hook, or size needed to obtain gauge

Weaving needle

Gauge:

8 dc (ch 2-sps) = 6"

Sizes:

Small (Medium, Large, X-large, XX-large)

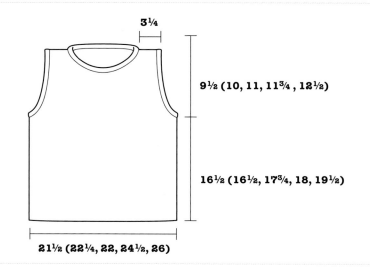

3¼

9½ (10, 11, 11¾, 12½)

16½ (16½, 17¾, 18, 19½)

21½ (22¼, 22, 24½, 26)

Directions

Body

Using color A, ch 131(136, 141, 151, 156).
With WSs facing, join to form a ring.

Rnd 1: Ch 2, 1 hdc in 2nd ch from hook, 1 hdc in ea ch around, join. [130(135, 140, 150, 155) sts]

Rnd 2: Ch 4 (count as 1st st now and throughout), *(sk next 2 sts, 1 dc in next st, ch 2), rep from * around, join. [43(45,47,51,52) dc]

Rnds 3–24(3–24,3–26,3–27,3–28): Ch 4, *(sk next 2 chs, 1 dc in next dc, ch 2), rep from * around, join. [43(45,47,51,52) dc] Fasten off.

Back

Sk 1st dc of previous rnd and join color A in 2nd dc.

Row 1: Ch 4, *(sk next ch sp, 1 dc in next dc, ch 2), rep from * 18(18,19,21,21) times, but do not ch 2 after the last dc. [20 (20,21,23,23) dc]

Row 2: Ch 4, turn, *(sk next ch sp, 1 dc in next dc, ch 2), rep from * 16(16,17,19,19) times, but do not ch 2 after the last dc. [18(18,19,21,21) dc]

Row 3: Ch 4, turn, *(sk next ch sp, 1 dc in next dc, ch 2), rep from * 14(14,15,17,17) times, but do not ch 2 after the last dc. [16(16,17,19,19) dc]

Row 4: Ch 4, turn, *(sk next ch sp, 1 dc in next dc, ch 2), rep from * 12(12,13,15,15) times, but do not ch 2 after the last dc. [14(14,15,17,17) dc]

Rows 5–9(5–10,5–11,5–12,5–13):
Ch 4, turn, *(sk next ch sp, 1 dc in next dc, ch 2), rep from * 10(10,13,15,15) times to end, but do not ch 2 after the last dc. [12(12,15,17,17) dc] Do not fasten off. You will now make the first back strap.

First back strap

Row 1: Ch 4, turn, *(sk next ch sp, 1 dc in next dc, ch 2), rep from * 3(3,5,5,5) times, but do not ch 2 after the last dc. [5(5,7,7,7) dc]

Row 2: Ch 4, turn, *(sk next ch sp, 1 dc in next dc, ch 2),rep from * 2(2,4,4,4) times, but do not ch 2 after the last dc. [4(4,6,6,6) dc]

Row 3: Ch 4, turn, *(sk next ch sp, 1 dc in next dc, ch 2), rep from * 1(1,3,4,4) times, but do not ch 2 after the last dc. [3(3,5,6,6) dc]

Row 4: Rep row 3. [3(3,5,6,6) dc] Fasten off.

Second back strap

With the front of the tank facing you, join color A in the corner of row 9(10,11,12,13) of the back.

Rep the directions for the first back strap. Fasten off.

With the front of the tank facing you, join yarn in the corner of the indicated row.

Front

With the RS facing you, join color A in 4th dc from the last dc of row 1 of the back.

Join yarn in the 4th st from the back

4 3 2 1

Join color A in the 4th double crochet from the back.

Row 1: Ch 4 (count as 1st st here and throughout, turn, *(sk next ch sp, 1 dc in next dc, ch 2), rep from * 18(18,19,20,21) times, but do not ch 2 after the last dc. [20(20,21,22,23) dc]

Row 2: Ch 4, turn, *(sk next ch sp, 1 dc in next dc, ch 2), rep from * 16(16,17,19,19) times, but do not ch 2 after the last dc. [18(18,19,20,21) dc]

Rows 3–8(3–9,3–9,3–10,3–10):
Ch 4, turn, *(sk next ch sp, 1 dc in next dc, ch 2), rep from * 14(14,15,17,17) times, but do not ch 2 after the last dc. [16(16,17,19,19) dc] Do not fasten off. You will now make the first front strap.

First front strap

Row 1: Ch 4, turn, *(sk next ch sp, 1 dc in next dc, ch 2), rep from * 5 times, but do not ch 2 after the last dc. (7 dc)

Row 2: Ch 4, turn, *(sk next ch sp, 1 dc in next dc, ch 2), rep from * 4 times, but do not ch 2 after the last dc. (6 dc)

Row 3: Ch 4, turn, *(sk next ch sp, 1 dc in next dc, ch 2), rep from * 3 times, but do not ch 2 after the last dc. (5 dc)

Row 4:	Ch 4, turn, *(sk next ch sp, 1 dc in next dc, ch 2), rep from * 2 times, but do not ch 2 after the last dc. (4 dc)
Row 5:	Ch 4, turn, *(sk next ch sp, 1 dc in next dc, ch 2), rep from * 1 time, but do not ch 2 after the last dc. (3 dc)

Continue for sizes Medium, Large, X-large, XX-large.

Row 6:	Rep row 5. (3 dc)

Continue for sizes Large, X-large, XX-large.

Row 7:	Rep row 5. (3 dc)

Continue for sizes X-large, XX-large.

Row 8:	Rep row 5. (3 dc)

Continue for size XX-large.

Row 9:	Rep row 5. (3 dc)

Second front strap

With the back of the tank facing you, join color A in the corner of row 8(9,9,10,10) of the front.

Rep the directions for the first front strap. Fasten off.

Joining the front and back straps

Using color A, turn the top inside out, match the top corners of the right front and back straps and join with a sl st seam. Fasten off.

Rep for the left front and back straps.

Neck

Turn the top RS out and ,with the front of the top facing you, join color A in the right inside shoulder seam. Work a sc edging around the neck hole. Join color B.

Rnds 1–2:	Ch 1, 1 sc in ea st around, join. [54(54,67,76,78) dc] Fasten off.

Armhole edging

Join color A at the sleeve seam of the armhole.
Work a hdc edging around the armhole, join. Join color B.

Rnds 1–2:	Ch 2, 1 hdc in ea st around, join. Fasten off. Rep for the other armhole. 54(54,67,76,78) Weave in all the ends.

Tune In

This mesh-style tunic is a great to wear throughout the year.
The elastic around the middle helps ensure a snug fit.

Materials needed:

450(500,550,600) yd or two 7-oz (198-g) skeins
of worsted-weight yarn in color A

200(250,300,350) yd or one 7-oz (198-g) skein
of worsted-weight yarn in color B

Size J/10 (6 mm) hook or size needed
to obtain gauge

Weaving needle

Round cord elastic

Gauge:

7 dc (ch 1 sps) = 4"

Sizes:

Small (Medium, Large, X-la

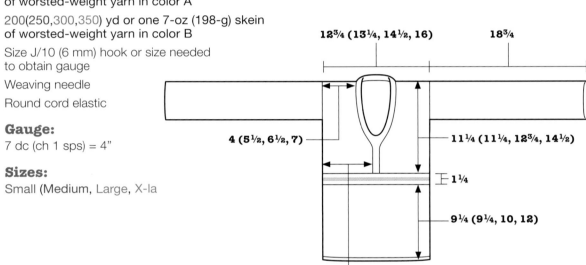

12¾ (13¼, 14½, 16)   18¾

4 (5½, 6½, 7)

11¼ (11¼, 12¾, 14½)

1¼

9¼ (9¼, 10, 12)

6 (7, 8½, 9¼)

Directions

Back

Using color B, ch 41(46,51,56), turn.

Row 1:   1 hdc in 2nd ch from hook, 1 hdc in ea ch to
         end. [40(45,50,55) sts] Join color A.

Row 2:   Ch 3 (count as 1st st now and throughout),
         turn, *(sk next st, 1 dc in next st, ch 1), rep
         from * to end, but do not ch 1 after last dc.
         [21(23,25,28) dc]

Rows 3–19(3–19,3–22,3–25):
         Ch 3, turn, *(sk next ch sp, 1 dc in next dc,
         ch 1), rep from * to end, but do not ch 1 after
         last dc. [21(23,25,28) dc] Fasten off.

Front panels

Using color B, ch 21(23,26,28).

Row 1:   1 hdc in 2nd ch from hook, 1 hdc in ea ch to
         end. [20(22,25,27) sts] Join color A.

Row 2:   Ch 3 (count as 1st st now and throughout),
         turn, *(sk next st, 1 dc in next st, ch 1), rep
         from * to end, but do not ch 1 after last dc.
         [11(12,13,14) dc]

Rows 3–11:	Ch 3, turn, *(sk next ch, 1 dc in next dc, ch 1), rep from * to end, but do not ch 1 after last dc. [11(12,13,14) dc]

Rows 12–19(**12–19**,12–22,12–25):
Ch 3, turn, *(sk next ch, 1 dc in next dc, ch 1), rep from * 8(9,9,10) more times, but do not ch 1 after last dc. [10(11,11,12) dc] Fasten off.

Make one more panel for a total of 2 panels.

Joining the panels
Using color A, with RSs facing, match up the sides of the right front panel with the back panel. Beginning at the bottom edge, join rows 1–11 with a sc seam. Fasten off.

Match the top corners. Join color A at the corner and join the panels with a sc seam. Fasten off.

Rep for left panel (WS of front panel will be facing outside).

Match up the sides and the top, and join with a single crochet seam.

Neck edging
With the front of the top facing you and the garment RS out, join color B at the bottom edge of the right panel and work a hdc edging around the neck.

Join color B at the bottom right corner of the right panel.

Rnd 1:	Ch 1, 1 sc in ea st around. [80(82,98,102) sts]
Rnd 2:	Ch 1, 1 sc in ea st around, join. [80(82,98,102) sts] Do not fasten off.

Joining the front panels
Turn the top inside out. Match the edges of the right and left front panels. With color B, starting at the bottom, join the panels with a sc seam for 10(13,16,18) sts. Fasten off.

Match the two front panels and join with a single crochet seam.

Border

Turn the top RS out. Using the right side seam as a guide, join color B at the bottom of the edging.

Rnd 1:   Ch 1, work 1 sc in ea st around, join. [87(90,97,103) sts]

Join color B at the bottom edging, using the right seam as a guide.

Weave elastic through rnd 1, then try the top on to see if the elastic is snug or loose enough. When it's the way you want it, cover the elastic.

Rnd 2:   Ch 1,1 sc in ea st around, join. [88(90,98,104) sts] Weave elastic through rnd 2 and cover.

Body

Join color A.

Rnd 1:   Ch 3, *(sk next st, 1 dc in next st, ch 1) rep from * around, join. [44(46,51,57) dc]

Rnds 2–15(2–15,2–16,2–18):
Ch 3, *(sk next ch, 1 dc in next dc, ch 1), rep from * around, join. [44(46,51,57) dc] Join color B.

Rnds 16–18(16–19,17–20,19–21):
Ch 1, 1 hdc in ea dc and ch sp around, join. [88(91,101,115) sts] Fasten off.

Sleeves

Join color A at bottom seam of armhole. Work a hdc edging around armhole.

Rnd 1:   Ch 3, *(sk next st, 1 dc in next st, ch 1), rep from * around, join. [19(19,21,25) dc]

Rnds 2–15:   Ch 3, *(sk next st, 1 dc in next dc, ch 1), rep from * around, join. [19(19,21,25) dc] Join color B.

Rnds 16–30(16–30,16–31,16–32):
Rep rnd 2. [19(19,21,25) dc]

Rnds 31–32(31–32,32–33,33–34):
Ch 1, 1 hdc in ea dc and ch st around, join. [36(36,40,50) sts] Fasten off. Rep for the other sleeve. Weave in all ends.

Top Shotta

This is a twist on the old-school turtleneck. It's as warm as it is cute.

Materials needed:

350(400,450) yd or one(two,two)
7-oz (198-g) skeins of worsted-weight yarn in color A

100 yd or one 7-oz (198-g) skein of worsted-weight yarn in color B

Size J/10 (6 mm) hook or size needed to obtain gauge

Weaving needle

Round cord elastic

Gauge:

10 hdc = 4"

Sizes:

Small (Medium, Large)

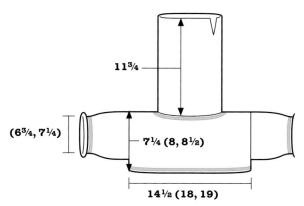

11¾

(6¾, 7¼)

7¼ (8, 8½)

14½ (18, 19)

Directions

Top

Using Color A Ch 91(101,111), join with WSs facing.

Rnd 1:   Ch 1, 1 hdc in ea ch around, join. [90(100,110) sts]

Rnd 2:   Ch 1 (Count as 1st st now and throughout), 1 hdc in 2nd st from hook, 1 hdc in ea st around, join. [90(100,110) sts]

Do not fasten off. Now you will begin the front of the top.

Front

Row 1:   Ch 1, 1 hdc in 2nd st from hook,1 hdc in next 41(46,51) sts. [43(48,53) sts]

You will begin to decrease in the next 2 rows by skipping last 2 sts.

Row 2:   Ch 1, turn, 1 hdc in 2nd st from hook, 1 hdc in next 39(44,49) sts. [41(46,51) sts]

Row 3:   Ch 1, turn, 1 hdc in 2nd st from hook, 1 hdc in next 37(42,47) sts. [39(44,49) sts]

Row 4:   Ch 1, turn, 1 hdc in 2nd st from hook, 1 hdc in next 31(36,41) sts, work 2 dec over the next 4 sts. [35(40,45) sts]

Row 5:   Ch 1, turn, 1 hdc in 2nd st from hook, 1 hdc in next 27(34,37) sts, work 2 dec over the last 4 sts. [31(36,41) sts]

Do not fasten off. For **small** and medium skip to side 1.

Continue for Large,

Row 6:   Ch 1, turn, 1 hdc in 2nd st from hook, hook, 1 hdc in ea st to end. (31(36,41) sts)

Side 1

Continue working to make strap.

Row 1:   Ch 1, turn, 1 hdc in 1st st from hook, 1 hdc in next 6(7,8) sts. (8,9,10) sts)

Rows 2-8(2-9,2-10):
           Ch 1, turn, 1 hdc in 2nd st from hook, 1 hdc in next 6(7,8) sts. (8,9,10) sts)

Fasten off.

Side 2

With front of top facing you, join yarn in the right corner.

Row 1:   Ch 1, turn, 1 hdc in 1st st from hook, 1 hdc
            in next 6(7,8) sts. (8,9,10 sts)

Rows 2-8(2-9,2-10):
            Ch 1, turn, 1 hdc in 2nd st from hook, 1 hdc
            in next 6(7,8) sts. (8,9,10 sts)

Back

With back of the top facing you, join color A in the 3rd st
from row 1 of the front.

Row 1:   Ch 1, 1 hdc in 1st st from hook, 1 hdc in
            next 41(46,51) sts. [(43,48,53) sts]

You will begin to decrease in the next 2 rows by skipping
last 2 sts.

Row 2:   Ch 1, turn, 1 hdc in 2nd st from hook, 1 hdc in next 39(44,49) sts. [41(46,51) sts]

Row 3:   Ch 1, turn, 1 hdc in 2nd st from hook, 1 hdc in next 37(42,47) sts. [39(44,49) sts]

Row 4-7:   Ch 1, turn, 1 hdc in 2nd st from hook, 1 hdc in next 35(40,45) sts. [37(42,47) sts]

Do not fasten off.

Side 1
Continue working to make side 1.

Row 1:   Ch 1, turn, 1 hdc in 1st st from hook, 1 hdc in next 6(7,8) sts. (8,9,10 sts)

Rows 2–8(2–9,2–10):
           Ch 1, turn, 1 hdc in 2nd st from hook, 1 hdc in next 6(7,8) sts. (8,9,10 sts)

Fasten off.

Side 2
With the back of the top facing you for small and large, join color A in the back right corner. for medium with front facing, join color A in the back right corner.

Row 1:   Ch 1, turn, 1 hdc in 1st st from hook, 1 hdc in next 6(7,8) sts. (8,9,10 sts)

Rows 2–8(2–9,2–10):
           Ch 1, turn, 1 hdc in 2nd st from hook, 1 hdc in next 6(7,8) sts. (8,9,10 sts)

Turn top inside out and join front and back sides with a sl st seam.

Fasten off.

front

Join the yarn in the 2nd st

Join yarn in the 2nd stitch from the front.

Joining the front and back
Turn the top WS out, match the corners of the straps, and join the front and back straps with a sl st seam.

Neck
Turn the top RS out. Join color A at the shoulder seam, work a sc edging around the neck hole, and join.

Rnd 1:   Weave elastic through the edging (don't pull it tight) and cover (see page 38). [84(92,99) sts]

Rnd 2:   Ch 1, (working in back loops only in this row only) 1 sc in 1st st from hook, 1 sc in ea st around, join. [84(92,99) sts]

Rnd 3:   Ch 1, *(1 sc in next 4 sts, 1 dec over next 2 sts), rep from * around, join. [71(77,82) sts]

Rnd 4:   Ch 1, *(1 sc in next 3 sts, 1 dec over next 2 sts), rep from * around, join. [57(62,66) sts]

Rnds 5–6: Ch 1, 1 sc in 2nd st from hook, ea st around, join. [57(62,66) sts]

Rnd 7: Weave elastic through last rnd, pulling so that the hole rests at the top of your collar bone. (Try the top on at this point to make sure your head fits through it. Adjust the elastic accordingly.) Cover the elastic.

Rnds 8–13: Rep rnd 5; do not join, instead, work in continuous rnds and join at the end of rnd 13. [57(62,66) sts]

Rnds 14–29: Ch 1, (work in front loops only for this row and the rest of the neck) rep rnd 5, do not join, instead, work in continuous rnds and join at the end of rnd 16. [57(62,66) sts]

You will now begin to make a split in the turtleneck.

Row 30: Rep rnd 5; (continue working in front loops); do not join. [57(62,66) sts]

Rows 31–40: Ch 1, turn, 1 sc in 2nd st from hook, 1 sc in ea st around, do not join. [57(62,66) sts] Fasten off. Join color B.

Ch 1, work a sc edging down both sides of the split.

Fasten off.

Work a single crochet edging in color B down both sides of the split in the turtleneck.

Sleeves

Join color A at the armhole seam, work a sc edging around, join.

Rnd 1: Ch 1 (count as 1st st here and throughout), 1 sc in 1st st from hook, 1 sc in ea st around, join. [36(39,45) sts]

Rnd 2: Ch 1, (work in back loops only in this row only) 1 sc in 2nd st from hook, 1 sc in ea st around, join. [36(39,45) sts]

Rnds 3–17(3–17,3–19): Ch 1, 1 sc in 2nd st from hook, 1 sc in ea st around; do not join, instead, work in continuous rnds and join with a sl st after rnd 17. [36(39,45) sts]

Rnd 18(18,20): Weave elastic through last rnd, pulling it to fit snug around your arm, then cover (see page 38).

Rnd 19–21(19–21,21–23): Rep rnd 3, joining after final rnd. Fasten off.

Rep for other sleeve.

Finishing

Weave elastic through the bottom edging of the top (don't pull it tight) and cover. Weave in all ends.

Warmittups

These legwarmers can be worn with a pair of heels and a skirt, shorts, or capri pants. They can even be worn on top of your jeans.

Materials needed:
450 yd or three 1.75-oz (50-g) skeins of sport-weight or worsted-weight yarn.

Size H/8 (5 mm) hook or size needed to obtain gauge

Weaving needle

Round cord elastic

Gauge:
Sport-weight yarn, 17 sc = 4"

Worsted-weight yarn, 14 sc = 4"

Directions

Ribbing 1
Ch 11.

Row 1:   1 sc in 2nd ch from hook, 1 sc in ea ch to end. (10 sts)

Rows 2–40:   Ch 1, turn (work in back loops only now and throughout ribbing), 1 sc in 2nd st from hook, 1 sc in ea st to end. (10 sts)

With RSs facing, join the two shorter sides with a sl st seam. At the end of the seam, ch 1 and work a sc edging around the side of the tube, join.

Weave elastic through the edging and cover (see page 38). Fasten off.

Work a sc edging on other side of the tube, then weave elastic through it and cover. Don't fasten off. Begin tube.

Tube
Rnd 1:   Ch 2, 1 dc in 2nd st from hook and in ea st around, join. (44 sts)

Rnds 2–15:   Ch 1, 1 dc in ea st around. Join. (44 sts)

At this point, you can add more dc rows if you need or want to make the leg warmers longer. Fasten off.

Ribbing 2
Ch 11.

Row 1:   1 sc in 2nd ch from hook, 1 sc in ea ch to end. (10 sts)

Rows 2–40:   Ch 1, turn (work in back loops only now and throughout ribbing), 1 sc in 2nd st from hook, 1 sc in ea st to end. (10 sts)

With RSs facing, join two shorter sides with a sl st seam.

At the end of the seam, ch 1, work a sc edging around, and join.

Weave elastic through the edging and cover. Fasten off.

Work a sc edging on other side of the tube, weave elastic through the edging and cover. Don't fasten off.

Joining the tube and ribbing 2
Turn the tube inside out.

With the WSs facing each other, join the edge of the ribbing and tube with a sl st seam.

Fasten off. Weave in all the ends.

Join the ribbing and tube with a slip-stitch seam.

Hoops

These hoop earrings can be made with metallic yarn for a dressier look or sport-weight yarn for a more casual look. Using cabone rings will make a small hoop and using metal bangles will give you a much larger flashier hoop (my personal favorite).

Materials needed:

50 yd or one 0.67-oz (19-g) skein of metallic or sport-weight yarn or crochet thread (if using thread, use two strands)

Size D/3 (3.25 mm) hook

Two 1" (7/25 mm) cabone rings

Two glass or plastic beads

Two fishhook wires

Tapestry needle, size 20

Fabric glue

Directions

Place a slip knot on a fishhook (if using crochet thread, use 2 strands, if using sport-weight or heavier yarn, use 1 strand). Work 37 sc (or however many sts are needed to cover the ring) around, join.

Ch 1 and fasten off, leaving 4" of yarn to secure the bead and hook later.

Using the 4" strand, secure 2 knots to the cabone ring, then add a bead by threading the remaining yarn through it. Tie a knot to secure the bead. Thread the yarn through the hole in the fishhook and secure with a knot.

Weave the remaining yarn back through the bead. Cut and glue the yarn. Rep for the other ring.

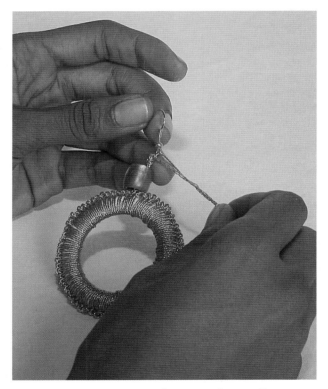

Secure the bead and hook with a weaving needle.

U Tube

Tube tops are one of my favorite things to wear in the summer. This top has elastic around the ribbing for a close fit. Accessorize with a belly chain, a bulky necklace, and some bangles to funk it up!

Materials needed:

240(320,360,450) yd or two(three,three,four) 7.9-oz (2.5-g) skeins of worsted-weight cotton yarn in color A

80(100,140,180) yds or one(one,two,two) 7.9-oz (2.5-g) skeins *each* of worsted-weight cotton yarn in colors B and C

Size H/8 (5 mm) hook or size needed to obtain gauge.

Stitch markers

Weaving needle

Round cord elastic

Gauge:

8 sc (ch 1 sps) = 4"

Sizes:

Small (Medium, Large, X-large)

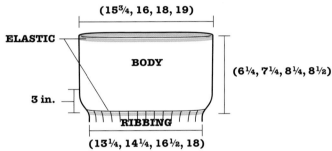

Directions

Ribbing

Using color A, ch 11.

Row 1:   1 sc in 2nd ch from hook, 1 sc in ea ch to end. (10 sts)

Rows 2–82(2–92,2–106,2–117):
Ch 1 (count as 1st st now and throughout), turn (work in back loops only now and throughout ribbing), 1 sc in 2nd st from hook, 1 sc in ea st to end. (11 sts)

With RSs facing, join 2 smaller sides of the ribbing with a sl st seam to form a ring.

Ch 1, then work a sc edging all the way around one side of the ribbing.

Work a single crochet edging around one side of the ribbing.

Weave elastic through the edging (don't pull it tight) and cover (see page 38). Fasten off.

Join color A to the other side of the ribbing, work a sc edging around, join.

Weave elastic through the edging (don't pull it tight) and cover. Do not fasten off. Now you'll begin the body.

Body

Rnd 1: Ch 1, 1 sc in 1st st from hook, 1 sc in next 2 sts, *(2 sc in next st, 1 sc in next 3 sts), rep from * around, join. [107(115,132,148) sts]

For Small and Medium, join color B. For Large and X-large, continue working with color A.

Rnd 2: Ch 2, 1 sc in 2nd st from hook, *(ch 1, sk next st, 1 sc in next st), rep from * around, join. [53(57,66,74) sts]

Rnds 3–5: Ch 2, *(sk next sc, 1 sc in next ch sp, ch 1), rep from * around; do not join. Use stitch markers to keep track of rnds. Join at the end of last rnd. [53(57,66,74) sts]

For Small and Medium, join color A. For Large and X-large, join color B.

Rnds 6–9: Rep rnd 3 [53(57,66,74) sts]

For Small and Medium, join color C. For Large and X-large, join color A.

Rnds 10–13: Rep rnd 3. [53(57,66,74) sts]

For Small and Medium, join color A. For Large and X-large, join color C.

Rnds 14–17: Rep rnd 3. [53(57,66,74) sts]

For Small and Medium, join color D. For Large and X-large, join color A.

Rnds 18–21: Rep rnd 3. [53(57,66,74) sts]

For Small and Medium, join color A. For Large and X-large, join color D.

Rnds 22–25: Rep rnd 3. [53(57,66,74) sts]

Fasten off for Small and Medium. Continue for Large and X-large.

Join color B.

Rnds 26–29: Rep rnd 3. [53(57,66,74) sts]

Join color A.

Rnds 30–33: Rep rnd 3. [53(57,66,74) sts]

Final rnd for all sizes:

Ch 1 (count as 1st st), 1 sc in ea sc and ch sp around, join. [108(114,132,148) sts] Do not Fasten off.

Trimming

Join color A.

Rnd 1: Ch 1, 1 sc in 1st st from hook, 1 sc in ea st and ch sp around, join. [98(105,118,131) sc]

Weave elastic through last rnd (don't pull it tight) and cover (see page 38). Fasten off. Weave in all the ends.

Resources

These are just a few resources that I use on a regular basis. The Internet has a vast array of information and lists of local crochet groups that you can join in your area.

Brands of Yarn

These are some of my favorite yarns because they are inexpensive, wash well, and have a great range of colors.

Berella®
www.bernat.com

Bernat®
www.bernat.com

Darice metallic craft cord®
www.darice.com

Hilos La Espiga nylon yarn®
www.hilosmega.com

Lion Brand Yarn®
www.lionbrand.com

DMC Mouline cross stitch yarn®

Needleloft craft cord®
www.uniekinc.com

Patons®
www.patonsyarns.com

Red Heart Soft®
www.herrschners.com

Sugar 'n Cream
www.sugarncream.com

Retailers

Local yarn stores usually have unique yarns that you can't find in the chain stores, but they are usually more expensive. Some of them have sales, and that is the best time to rack up. Check your yellow pages.

In thrift stores you can sometimes find vintage yarn in colors they don't make any more. You probably won't be able to find enough to make an entire project, but they are great to use as accent colors.

Hobby Lobby℠
www.hobbylobby.com

Jo-Ann Fabric & Crafts℠
www.joann.com

Michaels℠
www.michaels.com

Smiley's Yarns
www.smileysyarns.com

Wal-Mart℠
www.walmart.com

Mail-Order and Internet

Herrschners
www.herrschners.com
This mail-order catalog has great prices and a wonderful variety. It's also one of the few places I have seen that sells great colors of cotton yarn by the cone!

www.purplekittyyarns.com
www.purplekittyyarns.com
They sell yarn, needles, pattern books, and more.

Yarnmarket
www.yarnmarket.com
They have a great variety of textured and unique yarns.

Photo Locations

Laced Up Sneaker Boutique
572 Edgewood Ave.
Atlanta, GA 30312
404-230-5905
www.lacedup.biz

Negril Caribbean Cuisine
180 Auburn Ave. NE
Atlanta, GA 30303
404-827-9838
negrilcaribrestaurant.com

Clothing and Accessories Provided By

Convertible Bertt / Felix Meuon
The Store
228 Auburn Ave.
Atlanta, GA 30303
404-659-2338
www.convertiblebertt.com
www.felixmeuonline.com

Laced Up Sneaker Boutique
572 Edgewood Ave.
Atlanta, GA 30312
404-230-5905
www.lacedup.biz

NavyBlu
493-B Flat Shoals Ave.
Atlanta, GA 30316
404-230-5905

sewra g kidane
www.waistbeads.com

Sugar Britches
491 Flat Shoals Ave
Atlanta, GA 30316
404-522-9098
www.sugarbritchesatl.com

Whitney Mero
www.whitneymero.com

Yes Lioness
Marjorie Borgella
www.Yeslioness.com

Collecther Designs

Index

· · · · · · · · ·

Bold page numbers indicate photographs or illustrations, and *italicized* page numbers indicate tables. (When only one number of a page range is **bold** or *italicized*, illustrations or tables appear on one or more of the pages.)